# CONTENTS

S0-BST-465

AUTHORS' NOTES
*Dudley B. Woodard, Jr., Patrick Love, Susan R. Komives*

# Authors' Notes

The decade of the 1980s was a time of major reform in higher education. Most colleges revisited their mission statements (El-Khawas and Koop, 1996), general education requirements were reconceptualized, calls for campus community abounded, challenges to refocus on teaching were embraced, and much attention was devoted to reforming the experience of student athletes and enriching the experience of diverse students, especially students of color. The decade of the 1990s was a time to implement these reforms. Accountability measures demanded new outcome assessments, colleges reengaged with their communities, a quality agenda was advanced, the faculty role was examined, reactions to affirmative action threatened campus diversity, and attention shifted from teaching to learning. The public renewed its interest in the role of education in general and in the role of postsecondary education in particular. The future of a complex country called for new systems to approach difficult societal issues. Public leaders gathered for a conference at Wingspread, Wisconsin, in 1993 and posed the following challenge:

> What does our society need from higher education? It needs stronger, more vital forms of community. It needs an informed and involved citizenry. It needs graduates able to assume leadership roles in American life. It needs a competent and adaptable workforce. It needs very high quality undergraduate education producing graduates who can sustain each of these goals. It needs more first-rate research pushing back the important boundaries of human knowledge and less research designed to lengthen academic résumés. It needs an affordable, cost-effective educational enterprise offering lifelong learning. Above all, it needs a commitment to the American promise—the idea that all Americans have the opportunities to develop their talents to the fullest. Higher education is NOT meeting these imperatives [Wingspread Group, 1993, p. 2].

Our current challenge is the 2000s. How will higher education reengage with nation building (Edgerton, 1999) and make a much needed contribution to the public agenda? How will institutions reconceptualize their systems and structures to create enriched powerful learning experiences? How can student affairs professionals bring their wealth of knowledge about their experience with students to this process? This volume of *New Directions for Student Services* seeks to challenge readers to rethink what is currently happening, to imagine new futures, and to be courageous in engaging with other shareholders and stakeholders in meaningful conversation on these issues.

Most chapters in this issue use a common format to reveal what we are like now and shed light on what may need to be reexamined. The template that we use explores (a) assumptions, heresies, and myths, (b) themes and trends, (c) enduring principles and transcendent values, and (d) implications and challenges in order to help readers reflect on their assumptions. Einstein is said to have observed that today's problems cannot be solved by the paradigms that created them. Critically examining our assumptions may help us find new solutions to old problems as well as to the new challenges of the twenty-first century.

This volume is intended for those who have responsibility for the student experience in colleges and universities. Broadly stated, we seek to challenge student affairs administrators and other educators to use a systems approach in their work, to think about forming connections across the current functional areas, and to consider the broader group of shareholders and stakeholders who contribute to this experience.

## Content

Chapter One assesses the changing landscape of higher education. It analyzes the themes, issues, and trends from the past decade and explores the assumptions, myths, and heresies about higher education. Chapter Two explores how these trends influence student affairs practice and identifies the core values, principles, and theories that inform our practice, along with the faulty assumptions that shape student affairs culture. Chapter Three examines the changing nature of students in higher education. This chapter continues the exploration of diversification and highlights some of the more recent issues. Chapter Four explores changes in learning and development, notably the role that student affairs professionals must play in creating and sustaining these learning and developmental communities. Chapter Five presents reforms that are needed in organizational and management structures in order to accomplish these learning and developmental outcomes. Chapter Six considers new dimensions of student affairs financial capital, particularly the need to generate new and additional sources of funding and to take advantage of the marketplace without selling out our core principles. Chapter Seven describes and encourages active, collaborative leadership from student affairs professionals to help reshape structures and processes in higher education so they become more resilient and flexible in times of rapid change. Chapter Eight concludes the discussion by acknowledging that all professionals will need heightened skills and competencies to lead in these changing times.

## Exploring the Dark Corners

We admit from the outset that part of the task we have set for ourselves is to explore the dark corners of student affairs—the secrets we do not even want to admit to ourselves, no less to colleagues or anyone outside student affairs. We expect that a cursory reading of this text could be interpreted as a negative, pessimistic portrait of our profession. However, we believe that the text represents instead the great faith that we have in the profession of student affairs and the hope that we have for the future. We believe that it takes great courage to hold ourselves, as individuals and as a profession, up to a mirror in which our blemishes are evident and our ineffective, disempowering, or unflattering assumptions are revealed. It takes great courage to shed light into the dark corners of our practice and profession. We believe that as a profession we are strong enough and courageous enough to identify our weaknesses in order to address and eliminate them. As authors of this text, we do not hold ourselves separate from this endeavor. The process of planning, discussing, and writing this issue necessitated self-examination, and we found ourselves exhibiting the very assumptions we have identified in our profession in general. Writing this volume has been, at times, a humbling experience of personal exploration and discovery. However, it has also been a freeing, empowering, and strengthening process as well. That is our hope for the reader—that you will read and reflect on this text, experiencing the discomfort that comes with self-discovery as well as the renewal that comes with growth and the excitement of new self-learning. It is our further hope that as a self-empowering profession, we can realize the goals we have set for ourselves, those goals that in our moments of fear and doubt we believe may only be pipe dreams.

What this process will require is transformation. However, we are not talking about organizational transformation or transformational leadership. We are talking about self-transformation, transforming how we see our world—ourselves, our students, our roles, and our institutions. We need to transform our view of our students from the traditional focus on their psychological development to a focus on them as intellectual, social, and emotional individuals situated in a historical, cultural, and societal context. We need to transform our view of our role to one focused on the mission of the institution—student learning, growth, development, and success. And we need to transform our view of our institutions so that we see them as complex, holographic, dynamic cultures in which student affairs has an important role to play.

It is hard to imagine getting from here to there. These shifts are messy. They call on us, campus by campus, to engage in conversations about our local, shared futures and to bring good people together to determine how to respond to these challenges. This "bringing together" needs to happen at all levels of the organization. Former secretary of Health, Education, and Welfare and former president of Common Cause and the Independent Sector, John Gardner (1990), observed that we often are faced with wonderful opportunities brilliantly disguised as unsolvable problems. The challenges we face now in higher education, and all of those challenges that we will face in each subsequent decade, can be shaped and moved by our collective good thinking. Focused on enhancing the student learning and developmental experience, student affairs staff can facilitate a broad campus dialogue. Just start.

Dudley B. Woodard, Jr.
Patrick Love
Susan R. Komives
Authors

## References

Edgerton, R. "Education White Paper." Available on the Pew Charitable Trust Web site [http://www.pewtrusts.com]. Retrieved Sept. 2, 1999.

El-Khawas, E., and Koop, L. *Campus Trends 1996: Adjusting to New Realities*. Washington, D.C.: American Council on Education, 1996.

Gardner, J. W. *On Leadership*. New York: Free Press, 1990.

Wingspread Group on Higher Education. *An American Imperative: Higher Expectations for Higher Education*. Racine, Wis.: Johnson Foundation, 1993.

## Acknowledgments

In doing the research, writing, and editing for this resource volume, we were fortunate to have been assisted by several very competent, supportive graduate students. Many thanks to Christy Moran and Dawn DeToro, doctoral students in the Center for the Study of Higher Education, University of Arizona, for their help with the research and editing of the volume. Thank you, Christy, for your sharp editorial eye during the editing of the final draft. Two other students from the center assisted with the research, Anthony Berry, a first-year doctoral student, and Laura Hynes, a first-year master's student. Thank you, Anthony and Laura, for your thoroughness and support during the early stages of developing the plan for the volume and the chapter outlines. Much of the information related to the competencies of entrepreneurship, resource attraction, and organizing around learning and developmental outcomes was gathered by Kent State University graduate students in Patrick Love's course, Administration of Student Affairs. Thank you for your research contribution to the book, and we wish all of the students the very best for continued success in your graduate programs and in a wonderful profession—student affairs.

*DUDLEY B. WOODARD, JR. is professor of higher education at the Center for the Study of Higher Education at the University of Arizona, where he previously served as vice president for student affairs.*

*PATRICK LOVE is associate professor in higher education and student affairs at New York University. His scholarship focuses on organizational culture, student learning, spirituality, and the experiences of marginalized students in higher education.*

*SUSAN R. KOMIVES is associate professor and director of the College Student Personnel Administration graduate program at the University of Maryland. She is former vice president of Stephens College and of the University of Tampa.*

**1**

*Anticipating change in student affairs and developing new strategies to meet the challenges posed by change require an understanding of the current themes and trends in higher education. This chapter analyzes the higher education themes, issues, and trends from the past decade.*

# The Changing Landscape of Higher Education

During the next decade, the number of new and returning students to higher education will create a demand for academic and support services that cannot be met by simply doing what we have done in the past. We will need to find new solutions to meet this growing demand while addressing the perennial issues of access, cost, quality, and accountability. Increasing our capacity to serve the educational needs of a growing population without limiting essential programs will require that we clarify our priorities, create new partnerships, and design organizational structures that promote innovation while improving efficiency and reducing costs (2020 Commission on the Future of Post Secondary Education, 1998). Student affairs professionals will be challenged to rethink priorities and to develop new structures and strategies to support and serve students in a variety of educational settings. Rethinking our professional role requires an understanding of why and how higher education is changing and of the implications of this change for student affairs.

This chapter sets the context for the following chapters by reviewing the literature of the past decade in order to describe the changes in higher education and the likely future challenges and issues that will shape our institutions and our work. The first section analyzes some of the higher education position papers and commission documents that focus on the frequently cited themes and trends likely to continue as *change-drivers* (United Way of America's Strategic Institute, 1989) during the early part of the twenty-first century. These themes and trends are addressed throughout the volume but from different perspectives, such as leadership, organizational change, or the skills and competencies necessary to lead in these changing times. The second section describes how myths and heresies are used in this *New Directions* issue to help the reader examine and challenge beliefs and core assumptions about our institutions and our work. The final section addresses questions about the future practice of student affairs, which the reader may want to keep in mind while reading the remaining chapters.

## Themes, Trends, and Drivers from the 1990s

During the last half of this century, higher education went through several rapid, turbulent changes. The period following World War II is described as the Golden Age (Thelin, 1996). This was a period of unprecedented expansion at both the two-year and four-year levels in higher education. The 1960s and 1970s ushered in an era of optimism and youthful promise, focused on human and civil rights. This was also a period of great enrollment expansion, as the baby boomers began to attend postsecondary education in droves. The 1980s began the fiscal nightmare for higher education. Enrollments continued to grow, but financial support for higher education diminished as other societal needs, such as health care and social services, competed for shrinking funds. And the 1990s was a decade of restructuring higher education to address financial, quality, and accountability issues. It seems that the first decade of the new millennium will be characterized by efforts to transform our institutions so that they will be able to prepare students to meet what Russell Edgerton, the former president of the American Association for Higher Education and the director of the Pew Charitable Trusts in Higher Education, describes as "a growing accumulation of unsolved domestic problems, including family disintegration, loss of jobs, crime, and drugs" (Edgerton, 1999, p. 9).

The last fifty years have been remarkable for higher education. Despite fiscal, infrastructure, and accountability problems, enrollments continued to grow, graduation rates increased, and students found jobs! This certainly is a prosperous and proud past on which to build in the next century, providing a foundation from which to address the themes and challenges facing higher education during the next decade. This section highlights the major themes and trends of the past decade and identifies the social, political, and economic forces that may drive them. Each of these trends and themes has gained momentum and will need our attention in the next decade.

**The Engaged Institution.** The national report *Returning to Our Roots: The Engaged Institution* (Kellogg Commission on the Future of State and Land-Grant Universities, 1999) addresses the issue of the growing public frustration with our institutions—unresponsive, costly institutions that exercise little accountability. It describes an engaged institution as an institution that has "redesigned its teaching, research, and extension and service functions to become even more sympathetically and productively involved with their communities, however community may be defined" (p. I).

Edgerton (1999) speaks to the issue of nation building, "how to renew our social, political, and cultural life in the face of unprecedented change and a growing accumulation of unsolved domestic problems, including family disintegration, loss of jobs, crime, and drugs" (p. 9). Institutions are not perceived as being actively and visibly engaged in economic development and civic renewal. Edgerton sets an agenda for higher education that includes setting new aspirations for undergraduate education by encouraging institutions to take learning, pedagogy, and technology seriously; encouraging institutions to engage the public's agenda, especially regarding school reform; and encouraging ideals, policies, and practices that will develop an academic profession capable and interested in working toward these ends.

Clearly, the trend is toward building engaged institutions that will address societal issues and challenges. Community colleges are working with local businesses to develop training programs and methods by which they can update the skills of the local workforce. Research universities are building partnerships with industry, both locally and internationally, to enrich their research agendas and to secure funding. Institutions are supporting service learning, internships, and undergraduate research projects in order to integrate students into the local community.

**Enhanced Student Learning.** During the past decade, the public has demanded that more attention be paid to the learner. This call for learning-centered education was driven by a variety of factors, including the changing mix of students, the changing nature of the workforce, and changing pedagogies. This shift to a learning-centered education is necessary for a sustainable society; a sustainable society is "one that satisfies its needs without jeopardizing the prospects of future generations. It attempts to achieve growth and development without undermining the resources on which future prosperity depends" (Association of Governing Boards of Universities and Colleges, 1999, p. 23). The development of this type of society will require that student affairs professionals focus on supporting the academic mission of the institution in an attempt to deliver a learning-centered education in every functional area of the profession. In effect, student learning should be the desired outcome and goal of every student affairs program and activity.

We have learned much about how to create powerful learning environments (Chickering and Gamson, 1987). Institutions in general and student affairs divisions in particular will need the commitment and ability to redefine themselves in order to create learning environments that will be conducive to educating students to become engaged citizens, focusing less on individual needs and more on community needs. We need institutions that can negotiate market forces successfully to meet resource needs while preserving and building on core principles. In addition, we need to build and sustain academic environments that will prepare educated citizens who will contribute to both economic and societal needs. Student affairs professionals need to take an active stance in developing such environments.

**Knowledge as Capital.** One of the themes related to the evolving and dynamic world of higher education is the concept of *knowledge capital*. This refers to the notion that knowledge has become (or is becoming) the coin of the realm in today's society. Those with more knowledge are wealthier, more prestigious, and more powerful than those without knowledge. This concept interacts with, drives, and is driven by many issues, including economic considerations, globalization, and technology. The concept of knowledge capital implies that knowledge is a commodity or product. As such, it can be produced, measured, and distributed. It is therefore amenable to such administrative processes as coordination, automation, price and cost analyses, and efficiency and outcome assessment.

Higher education plays an important role in the creation and transmission of knowledge, but we should think of knowledge capital less as a commodity and more as a means to developing wisdom. Students need more than just knowledge as information. They need the ability to understand and apply the knowledge in order to gain wisdom. Wisdom refers to knowledge infused with experience, perspective, and content. Student affairs professionals should consider how they might structure student environments to provide the impetus for the development of wisdom.

**Accountability.** Accountability is an increasingly salient issue for higher education for a variety of reasons. First, funding sources, cost-effectiveness, and performance-based outcomes have become major concerns of the public, governing boards, and legislative bodies. Second, higher education institutions are being pressured to be more responsive to such market needs (Zemsky and Massy, 1995) as adequate preparation for the workforce and increased connections between higher education and the public (American Council on Education, 1998). Third, access, learning, and faculty productivity continue to be important issues in the academic realm. Combined, these have resulted in increased government skepticism and decreased public confidence in higher education (Gibbs, 1999). Higher education's affordability, access, and commitment to undergraduate education are all in question and most likely will continue to be scrutinized as long as fiscal, access, and quality-related problems remain.

Performance-based funding likely will occur more often due to fiscal crises in higher education, coupled with the new demands for accountability (Woodard and von Destinon, 2000). Programs and services that are not producing positive outcomes most likely will be cut. This will necessitate the consistent measuring and reporting of the benefits and outcomes of higher education (Institute for Higher Education Policy, 1998). An additional problem, however, is the identification of measurable outcomes. This too is an issue of controversy among higher education stakeholders who, due to their various value systems, emphasize certain outcomes more than other outcomes.

**Restructuring and Institutional Transformation.** Colleges and universities have faced intense pressure to change in new, different, and unfamiliar ways. In the 1970s and 1980s, the issue was how to do more with less. Today the issue is to rethink "basic operational definitions and assumptions about students and faculty, teaching and learning, resource allocation, and the ways in which scholarly questions are addressed and research findings applied" (Eckel, 1997, p. 1). In other words, the environmental demands have shifted from asking the university to do what it does for less money to asking the university to change what it does (Gumport and Prusser, 1995). This does not mean a change in basic functions such as teaching, research, and service but rather a change in how we think about what we do and then how we can do it differently to address the issues and challenges facing higher education and society successfully. Change will occur from examining basic underlying assumptions and from changing these assumptions to align with institutional and societal values and principles.

The increasing call for engagement in the community and outreach to the community will continue to transform our institutions in the areas of organization and governance (Kellogg Commission on the Future of State and Land-Grant Universities, 1999). The specialization of functions due to the changing nature of the workforce also has resulted in structural transformations and most likely will continue to do so in the future (Zemsky and Massy, 1995). Upcraft, Terenzini, and Kruger (1999) believe that technology will lead to new delivery systems. The need to decrease costs has resulted and most likely will continue to result in restructuring on college and university campuses.

Structural changes most likely will result in different methods of serving higher education constituents. For instance, restructuring may encourage collaboration across academic and student affairs divisional lines (Baxter Magolda and Terenzini, 1999). Franchises and outreach centers may be developed in response to the need for structural changes to better serve stakeholders (National Education Association, 1999).

Rhodes (1999) believes that higher education needs creative governance and trustee responsibility, along with aggressive, strong presidential leadership. Julius, Baldridge, and Pfeffer (1999) suggest that the key to making changes in higher education is to look at the organization and administration as well as the decision-making processes within institutions. Higher education leaders most likely will continue to search for an organizational paradigm that focuses on those served and that best meets their needs in the most cost-efficient manner.

**Rising Costs and Shifting Funding Sources.** The shifts in federal and state policy and the changes in economic conditions during the last thirty years (Breneman, 1993; Leslie, 1995) have resulted in the restructuring of higher education finances. For example, in the 1970s, most public institutions received more than 50 percent of their financial support from the state. Today it is less than 50 percent, and for most research universities, it is less than 30 percent. Higher education's share of the federal budget fell from 4 percent in 1975 to 2 percent in 1985 and has remained at this level throughout the 1990s (Carroll and Bryton, 1997). Tuition and fees in both the public and the private sector increased at a rate between two and three times the rate of inflation between 1980 and 1990, and by 1995, tuition and fees had increased by more than 100 percent compared with 1976 (Benjamin, 1998). Expressed in constant dollars, the cost of attendance (tuition, fees, and room and board) rose by 40 percent for public institutions and 60 percent for private institutions while per capita personal income increased only 18 percent during this same period (College Board, 1990). Demands for accountability and quality from higher-learning stakeholders have added to this fiscal pressure by requiring increased money for assessment, evaluation, and improvements in higher education.

The shifts in federal policies have produced similar effects in costs of attendance and sources of revenue. The introduction of Pell Grants, in 1972, was a major shift in federal policy, designed to keep the private sector competitive with the public sector and to reduce the public cost of higher education. Furthermore during the Reagan years, the Middle Income Assistance Act was dismantled in favor of targeting grants to low-income students and expanding loan programs for middle-income students. The shift to a high-tuition and high-aid policy during this period was designed to assist those students who needed financial support while also maintaining quality through the support provided by the tuition and fees paid by students from high-income families (Slaughter, 1997). Unfortunately, the rising cost of tuition hindered the success of this policy.

What then are the results of these fiscal pressures? First, a trend has developed in that institutions increasingly attain funding from private sources instead of from public sources. Students are more likely to take out loans than to receive grants and are more likely to pay high tuition and fees (Upcraft, Terenzini, and Kruger, 1999). In addition, privatization and downsizing are becoming more common methods of dealing with fiscal pressures in all areas of higher education (Komives, 1999). Finally, new entrepreneurial endeavors, such as contracting out services, developing research parks, and partnering with industry, are on the rise as institutions seek out new sources of revenue (Institute for Higher Education Policy, 1999).

**Market Responsiveness.** One of the major change-drivers of the next decade will be the influence of the marketplace. The marketplace refers to external influences on higher education and other areas of society, such as economic impacts, federal and state mandates, needs and desires of prospective students, and expectations of granting agencies. For many years, higher education, except for the community colleges and proprietary schools, operated without much influence from the marketplace. The last two decades have forced most institutions to look elsewhere for revenue to replace the decreasing state and federal dollars. The rise of for-profit higher education, the concept of students as consumers, and the demands from political entities have precipitated the need to consider higher education's degree of responsiveness to the marketplace.

A trend that exemplifies market responsiveness is the increasing link between private and public granting agencies. These relationships are attached to specific marketplace objectives, such as biotechnology, or to the development of operating systems for defense or private sector uses. A second trend is that of shifting from basic research to applied research. Institutions are being encouraged to form partnerships with the private sector in order for this to be successful (Slaughter, 1997). As the private–for-profit sector increases its financial investment in both public and private education, values increasingly will clash, and institutions of higher education may unwittingly or silently surrender to the interests of the marketplace investors.

**Globalization.** The forces of globalization—economic and financial, technological, political, and sociocultural—affect institutions of higher education no less than other societal institutions (Duncan, 1998). An increased focus on multidisciplinary global problems has resulted in increased pressure for higher education to provide solutions to both national and international problems (Kellogg Commission on the Future of State and Land-Grant Universities, 1999). Moreover the increased international trade and openness of economies have resulted in more competition in higher education—a competition for human resources, for faculty and students, as well as for physical resources such as research and development money.

One significant trend of globalization is that of changes in the curriculum, educational goals, and pedagogy in higher education. Orr (1993) emphasizes the importance of educating a global constituency that is scientifically literate, committed, and intellectually and politically active; students should become aware of the global society. Changes in the curriculum have included an increase in multidisciplinary programs as well as programs such as international education and environmental education (Orr, 1993). Globalization also has resulted in changes in the nature of academic research and funding for this research, as well as the transfer of research products and processes. Most likely, the global competition for resources will result in less money for higher education (Slaughter, 1997).

**Technology.** Higher education increasingly is becoming reliant on technology both in and out of the classroom. This increased salience of technology can be seen in various realms of higher education, including administrative, academic, and student services areas. In addition, there continues to be growth in the areas of virtual and distance education. This increased use of technology has affected pedagogical methods and has introduced new fiscal challenges (Upcraft, Terenzini and Kruger, 1999).

Although technology may increase access to higher education (Edgerton, 1999; Gubernick and Ebeling, 1997), the organizational structure of higher education may continue to change. For instance, college and university campuses are becoming less residential as students no longer are required to be present physically in classroom situations.

In addition, it is clear that the role of faculty is changing in response to the increased use of technology. Besides mastering new tools of technology, faculty will be forced to reevaluate the entire process of teaching and learning (Ogilvy, 1994). Perceived problems of the impact of technology on higher education include potential legal issues, less face-to-face interaction with students, and the perpetuation of social-class inequities (Ogilvy, 1994; Upcraft, Terenzini, and Kruger, 1999). Student affairs professionals will need to anticipate and respond to such challenges.

**Diversity.** Our society is no doubt becoming increasingly global and diverse, and this diversity in the society is being mirrored in higher education. There are increasing numbers of females, minorities, and students with disabilities who are gaining access to higher education. In addition, the renewed emphasis on vocational training has resulted in students attending higher education on a part-time or intermittent basis (Edgerton, 1999). Many of these students are over the age of twenty-five and are entering higher education with diverse backgrounds, attitudes, and motivations toward learning as well as with mental and psychological issues (Baxter Magolda and Terenzini, 1999).

Higher education will need to respond to this increasing diversity by becoming more inclusive and by developing caring, supportive environments (Rhodes, 1999). New services and programs will need to be designed and implemented in order to respond to the variety of student needs that exist in a multicultural environment. Methods of pedagogy such as independent study programs may be used more frequently as many students struggle to balance school with their need to work full-time.

Diversity also will influence faculty and administrators in institutions of higher learning. Just as the student body is becoming more diverse, so are the faculty and administrators (Komives, 1999). Women and minorities are gaining increasing numbers of positions as faculty members, although most of these positions are part-time (Finkelstein, Seal, and Schuster, 1998).

Higher education will need to respond by providing opportunities for faculty development in the area of multiculturalism and diversity. Assessments and evaluations will need to be undertaken in order to determine whether or not institutions are meeting the needs of the diverse constituents served. New methods of determining financial aid eligibility may need to be developed in order to respond to the complexities of the backgrounds and situational factors represented by an increasingly diverse student body.

In summary, the themes and trends mentioned in this section will most likely continue to generate new trends in the future. The implications of these themes and trends for the next decade must not go unnoticed. We must begin to think actively about how the higher education learning environment needs to be organized to best meet the needs of students in the midst of these transforming trends.

## Myths and Heresies

Before we think about how to restructure our learning environments to enhance student success and to engage students in lifelong learning and responsible community citizenship, it is useful to examine some of the myths and heresies held by student affairs professionals about higher education and more specifically about the practice of student affairs. Understanding these myths and heresies will help us think about the core assumptions and principles of our institutions; this is a prerequisite for developing strategies and tactics to create and sustain learning environments that promote lifelong learning and civic engagement.

*Myths* are beliefs that are based on tradition as opposed to evidence. Although inaccurate, myths are part of the culture of institutions or professional fields. They are used to socialize newcomers and are accepted as unquestionably true by members of that culture. Our tendency is to behave as if these myths are true when, in fact, they are false. Myths can be powerful, political institutional sagas that serve as institutional fire walls against change. Helping others understand the nature of myths, while still drawing on the power of those myths, can be a useful change strategy. We argue here that some unquestioned beliefs in higher education and student affairs actually are myths. A few examples of what we believe to be myths are the following: higher education is an equitable enterprise, students have access and choice, students are being prepared adequately for the world of work, and student affairs professionals focus on the whole student. Other myths will be discussed in subsequent chapters.

In contrast, *heresies* are opinions or assertions that are at odds with widely held beliefs or accepted practices. These are controversial or unorthodox beliefs that contradict accepted truths held by a group of people. The weight of evidence as filtered through our assumptions is overwhelmingly against heresies; this explains why heresies are counter to strongly held assumptions. Using heretical positions as a way to engage discussion on issues can be effective as long as real change and not martyrdom is the objective. For example, to state that student affairs professionals are territorial and self-serving is not only heretical but also harsh. Yet a closer examination of behaviors may reveal professionals who are more interested in defining boundaries than in crossing them, as a means to preserve and protect the existing programs and services in a student affairs division.

Myths help us deal with difficult work situations and questions of identity (Morgan, 1997), and heresies allow us to rationalize our behavior as critics or institutional outliers. Myths and heresies also help sustain and change institutional culture. A thorough understanding of both will help us decide which to leave alone and which to challenge. Throughout this volume, we use myths and heresies as tools to challenge the reader to examine and reflect on institutional and professional beliefs and core assumptions.

## Creating Our Future in Student Affairs

What is remarkable about the major themes and trends described earlier in the chapter and the myths, heresies, and assumptions presented in subsequent chapters are their durability and consistency. These are the issues that have dominated higher education for the past three decades and will continue to do so in the foreseeable future. Issues of cost, access, quality, and accountability have been the major issues challenging higher education. What is new, but no less important, is the interplay between these issues and the domestic and international marketplace. Market forces, globalization, and technology have become significant external determinants of what happens inside the academy. Many worry that higher education may lose its identity as an institution charged with generating knowledge free of private interests and promoting learning and character development in its students as a consequence of the interplay among these issues and change-drivers.

Understanding the dynamic interplay among these issues and change-drivers is essential for student affairs professionals in anticipating how to sustain our professional core values and principles while developing new strategies and tactics to succeed and meet the needs of our students.

The following chapters will address how student affairs professionals can think about refining our roles and organizational structures to address this new reality while remaining faithful to the core principles and values that have served our profession so well during the last hundred years. As you read the rest of this resource volume, use the following questions for self-examination and reflection. Use these questions to probe institutional beliefs and core assumptions and to think about how you can transform your institution, division, or department to meet the challenges posed by these themes and trends.

- How will institutions transform themselves to meet the public agenda?
- How will we reshape our practice to meet changing conditions and the changing needs of our students?
- What are desired student affairs outcomes, and how do those outcomes relate to institutional outcomes?
- How will our institutional priorities and values change as a result of market influence and control?
- How do the perspectives and worldviews of ethnicity, class, and gender inform creative approaches to change?
- How will programs and services deemed central to sustaining core institutional values and principles be funded?
- How do we shape technology to influence student affairs practice, student development, and learning and not merely react to technological changes?
- How well can we prepare our students to live in an economically interdependent society?

• How will our Western conceptions of social justice and equality be changed?

## References

American Council on Education. *On Change: En Route to Transformation.* American Council on Education Occasional Paper Series. Washington, D.C.: American Council on Education, 1998.

Association of Governing Boards of Universities and Colleges. *Ten Public Policy Issues for Higher Education in 1999 and 2000.* Washington, D.C.: Association of Governing Boards of Universities and Colleges, 1999.

Baxter Magolda, M. B., and Terenzini, P. T. "Learning and Teaching in the 21st Century: Trends and Implications for Practice." In C. S. Johnson and H. E. Cheatham (eds.), *Higher Education Trends for the Next Century: A Research Agenda for Student Success.* Washington, D.C.: American College Personnel Association, 1999.

Benjamin, R. "Looming Deficits: Causes, Consequences, and Cures." *Change,* 1998, 30(2), 13–17.

Breneman, D. *Higher Education: On a Collision Course with New Realities.* Association of Governing Boards of Universities and Colleges, Occasional Paper no. 22. Washington, D.C.: Association of Governing Boards of Universities and Colleges, 1993.

Carroll, S., and Bryton, E. *Higher Education's Fiscal Future.* Washington, D.C.: American Council on Education, 1997.

Chickering, A. W., and Gamson, Z. F. *Principles for Good Practice in Undergraduate Education.* (special insert to the *Wingspread Journal*) Racine, Wis.: Johnson Foundation, June 1987.

College Board. *Trends in Student Aid: 1980 to 1990.* New York: College Entrance Examination Board, 1990.

Duncan, T. *As They See It: The Meaning of Globalization for Theological Educators in North America and Their Proposals for Institutional Response.* Unpublished manuscript, 1998.

Eckel, P. "Capturing the Lessons Learned: The Evaluation Process for the American Council on Education-Kellogg Project on Leadership and Institutional Transformation." Paper presented at the Association for the Study of Higher Education annual meeting, Albuquerque, 1997.

Edgerton, R. "Education White Paper." Available on the Pew Charitable Trust Web site [http://www.pewtrusts.com]. Retrieved Sept. 2, 1999.

Finkelstein, M. J., Seal, R. K., and Schuster, J. H. *The New Academic Generation: A Profession in Transformation.* Baltimore: Johns Hopkins University Press, 1998.

Gibbs, A. "Changing Government Roles Relative to Higher Education." In C. Johnson and H. Cheatham (eds.), *Higher Education Trends for the Next Century: A Research Agenda for Student Success.* Washington, D.C.: American College Personnel Association, 1999.

Gubernick, L., and Ebeling, A. "I Got My Degree Through E-Mail." *Forbes,* Jan. 16, 1997. [http://www.forbes.com/97/0616/5912084a.htm].

Gumport, P. J., and Prusser, B. "A Case of Bureaucratic Accretion: Context and Consequences." *Journal of Higher Education,* 1995, 66(5), 493–520.

Institute for Higher Education Policy. *Reaping the Benefits: Defining the Public and Private Value of Going to College.* Washington, D.C.: Institute for Higher Education Policy, 1998.

Institute for Higher Education Policy. *The Tuition Puzzle: Putting the Pieces Together.* Washington, D.C.: Institute for Higher Education Policy, 1999.

Julius, D. J., Baldridge, J. V., and Pfeffer, J. "A Memo from Machiavelli." *Journal of Higher Education,* 1999, 70(2), 113–133.

Kellogg Commission on the Future of State and Land-Grant Universities. *Returning to Our Roots: The Engaged Institution.* Washington, D.C.: National Association of State Universities and Land-Grant Colleges, 1999.

Komives, S. R. "The Changing Nature of Work in Higher Education." In C. S. Johnson and H. E. Cheatham (eds.), *Higher Education Trends for the Next Century: A Research Agenda for Student Success.* Washington, D.C.: American College Personnel Association, 1999.

Leslie, L. "What Drives Higher Education Management in the 1990s and Beyond? The New Era in Financial Support." *Journal of Higher Education Management,* 1995, *10*(2), 5–16.

Morgan, G. *Images of Organization.* (2nd ed.) Thousand Oaks, Calif.: Sage, 1997.

National Education Association. "The Future of Higher Education: Market-Driven and Quality-Driven." [http://www.nea.org/he/future/market.html]. 1999.

Ogilvy, J. "The Information Revolution." *On the Horizon,* 1994, *2*(4), 1–5.

Orr, D. W. "Educating a Constituency for the Long Haul." *On the Horizon,* 1993, *2*(1), 1–5.

Rhodes, F. Address to the Association of Governing Boards National Conference on Trusteeship. Washington, D.C.: Association of Governing Boards of Universities and Colleges, 1999.

Slaughter, S. "Who Gets What and Why in Higher Education? Federal Policy and Supply-Side Institutional Resource Allocation." Presidential speech to the Association for the Study of Higher Education, Memphis, May 1997.

Thelin, J. R. "Historical Overview of American Higher Education." In S. R. Komives and D. B. Woodard, Jr. (eds.), *Student Services: A Handbook for the Profession.* (3rd ed.) San Francisco: Jossey-Bass, 1996.

2020 Commission on the Future of Post Secondary Education. "Learning for Life." [http://www.governor.wa.gov]. 1998.

United Way of America's Strategic Institute. *What Lies Ahead: Countdown to the 21st Century.* Alexandria, Va.: United Way of America, 1989.

Upcraft, M. L., Terenzini, P. T., and Kruger, K. *Higher Education Trends for the Next Century: A Research Agenda for Student Success.* Washington, D.C.: American College Personnel Association, 1999.

Woodard, D. B., Jr., and von Destinon, M. *Weathering the '90s.* Unpublished manuscript, 2000.

Zemsky, R., and Massy, W. F. "Expanding Perimeters, Melting Cores, and Sticky Functions: Toward an Understanding of Our Current Predicaments." *Change,* Nov.–Dec. 1995, *27,* 41–49.

**2**

*This chapter explores how the higher education themes and trends influence student affairs practice and identifies the core values, principles, and theories that inform our practice, along with the faulty assumptions that shape student affairs culture.*

# Reframing Our Thinking, Reshaping Our Practice

Change is and has been a fact of life in American higher education. Vaill (1996) describes the state of our society as "permanent white water" (p. xiv). This notion is meant to move us from the assumption that the "normal" process of organizational life is change-stability-change-stability. Those holding this outdated assumption spend their time waiting for a break where they can catch their breath. That break is not coming. As described in Chapter One, American higher education continually responds to shifting trends and emerging issues.

Student affairs professionals must be about the business of making themselves aware of what is happening around them in terms of society and higher education, discovering assumptions about who they are and what they do, transforming outdated assumptions, and shaping student affairs practice to address the changes and to take into account new assumptions. This process requires *double-loop learning* (Argyris, 1991). Double-loop learning means that practitioners not only learn from their mistakes (*single-loop learning*) but also learn to identify disempowering and faulty assumptions about the context and situation in which they are working. An example of single-loop learning is learning from staff member feedback about running more efficient staff meetings. Double-loop learning would include questioning and assessing whether you should even be having a staff meeting or if the objectives of the staff meeting might be better met in other ways. In this chapter, we identify negative assumptions by discussing heresies and myths about student affairs culture. These negative assumptions are disempowering and concern who we are, our roles, and our relationships. We do also believe, however, that there are values and principles that must persist in their influence on student affairs work and that there are lessons that have been learned in the first century of the student affairs profession that will continue to serve the field well in the next. After presenting and discussing the myths, heresies, and principles, we discuss the trends and issues identified in Chapter One. These trends and issues strongly represent the context in which student affairs professionals conduct their work as the new century dawns. Finally, we consider the degree to which student affairs is responding to these changes and what else may need to be done.

## Myths and Heresies

As indicated in the Authors' Notes, we attempt to challenge our readers by identifying myths and heresies as a method of revealing subconscious views and beliefs that professionals hold about themselves, their work, students, others at work in institutions of higher education, and the institutions themselves. We recognize that this exercise results in asserting generalizations about student affairs professionals and about the field in general. It is our hope that readers will not dismiss them out of hand but rather will use them as a form of self-examination. Identifying and examining heresies is a brutal form of self-examination. It is also a potentially transforming and empowering form of self-examination. Individuals are never so firmly trapped and constrained as by their own disempowering assumptions. But on reflection and identification we can unlearn these assumptions. Undiscovered and unexamined assumptions are part of who we are. They can only become distinct from the self when they are discovered and identified. In fact, the first *heresy* that we assert is that *student affairs professionals tend not to challenge their own assumptions about their knowledge, beliefs, values, students, faculty, and organizational functioning.* In a field focused on learning and development, stating something that is apparently antidevelopmental must be considered a heresy. But student affairs professionals are not alone in failing to challenge assumptions. The fact is that assumptions are taken-for-granted beliefs that influence us outside our consciousness. As we become socialized to the culture of the field of student affairs, we are less and less likely to challenge what we know and believe about students, faculty, our roles, and our institutions. Yet if the information we provide in this volume is to be of any use to the reader, discovering and challenging our own assumptions is imperative.

Our most extreme *heresy* is the assertion that *student affairs, as a profession, has developed a self-marginalizing, disempowering, self-pitying culture, resulting in student affairs professionals who have a victim mentality and a sense of powerlessness.* This is the most painful heresy to assert as we recognize that it is not a flattering self-portrait. One might ask, how could this be true? One would think that student affairs is all about combating marginalization, creating inclusive communities, and empowering others. We do not disagree; however we also believe that far too many student affairs profession-als marginalize and disempower themselves and are, at times, even self-pitying. Consequently, we believe that this heresy is in fact a basic current truth about the field of student affairs. It is also our belief that in order to meet the challenges represented by the trends noted in Chapter One, stu-dent affairs professionals must realize the veracity of this statement and work to change so that it will no longer be true.

The fact that as a field student affairs is self-marginalizing, when com-pared with other professions, should not come as a surprise. Although it is an essential partner, student affairs is not at the center of the mission of aca-deme. When our profession is not central to the purpose of a corporate entity, a dynamic occurs that can result in the tendency to push ourselves further to the margins in response to the actions of those at the center and in response to recognizing our plight (Roberts, 1983). The same can be seen in other professions. For instance, in the health care field, although nurses are partners in the process, doctors are the "main show." Like student affairs, the nursing profession has suffered from the "woe is we" phenome-non (Arena and Page, 1992; Bent, 1993; Whelan, 1996) and is making strides to combat this tendency (Whelan, 1996; Woolf, 1984). The notion that if we are not an equal partner, we feel devalued is a real phenomenon for different levels of professionals in any setting. In describing nurses, Woolf indicated that low self-esteem or low self-worth is problematic because a positive self-image is necessary for believing one can influence one's future. The challenge is to recognize this self-marginalizing tendency and to counteract it. Our point is that when the internalized sense of learned helplessness is transformed to a sense of self-empowerment, and the field claims a place in the academy to do the good work that is needed, then the way that student affairs is viewed and treated by others is transformed as well.

This discussion leads us and is related to one of the *myths* of our pro-fession: *if student affairs is not an equal partner in the work of the institution, then the field is being devalued.* What is difficult to comprehend is that we can be a "lesser" (that is, less central) partner yet still be vital to the mission of the institution. Again looking at other professions, we need only ask sur-geons how they would accomplish their work without an anesthesiologist, an operating-room technician, or a myriad of assistants in order to get a good idea of this concept. Although student affairs professionals are not fac-ulty, they still conduct important educational, developmental, administra-tive, service-related tasks, without which the institution could not function, and certainly the influence on the effectiveness of the student experience would be felt.

A related *myth* is that *student affairs professionals focus on the whole stu-dent.* Many student affairs professionals might argue that they deal holisti-cally with students. Research, however, indicates that student affairs, as a profession, has tended to focus on the psychosocial experience of college students (Kuh, Bean, Bradley, and Coomes, 1986). Given the emerging prominence of a focus on student learning, this indeed may be changing. However, it is our observation that practitioners in such traditional areas of student affairs as residence life and student activities tend *not* to do the following:

- Inquire about students' studies and academic progress.
- Formally or informally promote good study habits among students.
- Help students connect what they are learning in the classroom with their out-of-class experiences.
- Encourage study groups, study time, or confront students who appear overly involved in social activities to the detriment of their studies.
- Know which students are succeeding academically and which students are struggling.
- Confront the anti-intellectual student culture that pervades so many institutions.

A corollary to this *myth* is that *student affairs can only focus on holistic development by collaborating with faculty and academic affairs.* On the surface, casting this as a myth appears troublesome, especially in this era of building bridges between faculty and student affairs professionals, creating collaborations between academic and student affairs, and connecting in-class and out-of-class activities. However, think about this: For how many of the activities cited previously are faculty or academic affairs needed? None. We are concerned about the current taken-for-granted, prevailing belief that in order to meet the learning and intellectual needs of students effectively, student affairs professionals need to create partnerships with faculty and to connect student affairs with academic affairs and that until those partnerships are created, we cannot address students' holistic learning and developmental needs. We need to be clear: collaborating with faculty and academic affairs is important and laudable. However, if that is not done, it is no excuse for not meeting or attempting to meet the learning and intellectual needs of all students.

Finally, an organization-related *heresy* is that *student affairs professionals tend not to look at the big picture.* We argue that the tendency for student affairs professionals at traditional four-year colleges and universities is to focus on issues strictly defined as in the purview of student affairs, and rarely do we look beyond the institution. Even those professionals whose jobs include working beyond the boundaries of the campus (for example, Greek life, community service) tend to keep their focus on the issues specifically related to their task.

## Enduring Principles and Transcendent Values

While addressing the dynamic environment in which student affairs exists and recognizing the necessity for changing and transforming to meet the challenges of a new century, we also acknowledge that there are enduring principles and values that transcend this time period and provide an element of continuity in this experience of change and transition. A review of several of the documents focusing on the field of student affairs that have been produced during the last sixty years, such as *The Student Personnel Point of View* (American Council on Education, 1937, 1949), *The Student Learning Imperative* (American College Personnel Association, 1994), the Council of Student Personnel Associations in Higher Education statement (1975), *A Perspective on Student Affairs* (National Association of Student Personnel Administrators, 1987), and *Good Practice in Student Affairs* (Blimling and Whitt, 1999), demonstrates that these appear to be the ideals toward which we strive as a profession. Identifying them as ideals implies the recognition that they are not necessarily the lived reality or basic assumptions of even the majority of student affairs professionals. However, they are presented here to set the stage for future discussion:

- A belief in the dignity, uniqueness, potential, and worth of each individual.
- A belief that our role is to enhance student learning and student development.
- A belief in the development of the whole person, including the importance of intellectual, social, emotional, ethical, and spiritual elements.
- A belief that learning occurs in diverse places and in diverse ways.
- A belief that ultimately students must take responsibility for their own learning.
- A belief in individuation and community, recognizing the powerful role of community in learning and development.
- A belief in caring for students by setting and communicating high expectations for learning and behavior.
- A belief in communities where diversity is desired, where mutual respect is expected, and where ideas and assumptions are to be explored and questioned.
- A belief in encouraging conversation and communication, instead of stifling it, no matter how offensive the ideas may be to some.
- A belief that the mission of student affairs flows from the mission of the institution.
- A belief that higher education and student affairs have roles in assisting in the transformation of our society into a learning society.

These are the ideals and the principles that should play a significant role in how student affairs professionals in particular and the profession in general face the challenges of a new century. However, we argue that there are additional values and principles that should guide our practice, values that are often ignored in the documents reflecting the national conversation of our profession. These values and principles have to do with the administrative and managerial aspects of virtually all student affairs positions. They are drawn from a variety of sources, including *Good Practice in Student Affairs* (Blimling and Whitt, 1999):

- A belief that professionals must exhibit individual initiative and seek to collaborate with colleagues and others.
- A belief in personal and departmental self-examination, reflection, and continual improvement of administrative practice.

Although all of these principles must play a role in the work of student affairs, the next section highlights specific principles related to the trends.

## The Student Affairs Response to Higher Education and Societal Trends

In this section, we begin to address the higher education trends identified in the first chapter and to discuss how they are related to student affairs and how student affairs currently is responding to them. We also put forward the implications and offer suggestions for how student affairs professionals need to be responding to them. Each of the chapters in the rest of this volume deals more specifically with the trends; this section deals with them generally. To assist with the task of comparing the trends with current practice, Love and others (2000) investigated issues of importance to student affairs by examining the profession's discourse as represented by the topics in professional organizations' newsletters, periodicals, conference programs, keynote addresses, Web sites, and other information. The discourse study analyzed more than a thousand textual units (such as individual newsletter articles, conference programs, and Web pages) and identified fifteen major categories. The categories and their percentage of representation in the discourse were student learning (29.3 percent), multiculturalism and diversity (16.2 percent), social issues (10.4 percent), student affairs (9.6 percent), collaboration (9.1 percent), leadership (6.7 percent), technology (5.1 percent), assessment (2.7 percent), Greeks (1.7 percent), involvement (1.5 percent), legal issues (1.4 percent), funding (1.2 percent), retention (1.2 percent), financial aid (1.1 percent), and international education (1.0 percent). Student learning stands out as a dominant theme in the discourse of student affairs. Other strongly represented topics included multiculturalism and diversity, general social issues (for example, alcohol, drugs, gambling, violence), general student affairs–related issues (for example, professional organizations, professional development, career and job search), collaboration, leadership, and technology.

In the following discussion, we compare the trends discussed in Chapter One with the topics in the discourse of student affairs and with the trends identified in *Higher Education Trends for the Next Century* (Johnson and Cheatham, 1999), produced by the American College Personnel Association (ACPA) Senior Scholars. The ACPA document addresses trends of importance to student affairs practice and research and proposes responses to eight trends—improve access and success for diverse students, respond to the rising cost of higher education, focus on learning and teaching, respond to and keep abreast with technology, respond to the changing nature of work in higher education, recognize the importance of collaboration and partnerships, respond to the calls for accountability, and respond to changing government roles vis-à-vis higher education (see Table 2.1).

Table 2.1 compares the three data sets, sorted from areas of greatest congruence to those of least congruence and includes topics that are absent from one or more of the lists. Each column lists both the trends and topics as well as the issues discussed in each section. In the student affairs discourse column, the major categories are rated according to their strength. Also included with these major categories are the subcategories identified within them. The subcategories are not rated but help define the major category. The internal issues and subcategories across each row have been aligned where appropriate with similar or corresponding trend topics for clearer comparison purposes.

Six items emerge for which there is at least some congruence among the lists. The most strongly connected issues across the three lists are student learning, multiculturalism and diversity, collaboration, and technology. The changing nature of work and accountability also appear to have similarities. Multiculturalism and diversity and student learning are the two strongest categories in the discourse of the field. Technology was judged to be of moderate strength, and collaboration was considered a strong category.

**Increased Focus on Student Learning.**  All three lists mention student learning. In fact, it is the largest portion in the discourse of the student affairs field, representing almost 30 percent of the topics identified. Within the categories, there are similar foci on specifying and assessing outcomes of student learning and on shifting pedagogical methods. Not surprisingly, the discourse of the field also focuses on such practice-oriented topics as academic advising, the first-year experience, and service learning. The issue of student learning is prominent in the list of core values. This focus on student learning is addressed in greater depth in Chapter Four.

**Multiculturalism and Diversity.**  Again all three lists have a specific focus on the topic of diversity. All three lists also define as an element of diversity the continuing diversification and changing needs of the student body, which is the specific focus of Chapter Three. There is also some emphasis in all three lists on diversity of context. As you will recall, Chapter One focuses on the diversity of institutions throughout higher education (as represented in the list in column one), whereas the other two lists speak more generally to diverse environments (which can be intrainstitutional as well as interinstitutional) and to creating inclusive communities. The importance and desirability of diversity of students is quite specific in the list of core values; however, issues of institutional diversity are less so.

Related to the topic of institutional diversity, it is important for student affairs leaders and practitioners in four-year institutions to realize the wealth of knowledge and practical experience that professionals in community colleges and nontraditional institutions and sectors (for example, student

# Table 2.1. Comparison of Trends and Discourse Topics

| Higher Education and Societal Trends | American College Personnel Association Trends | Student Affairs Discourse Topics[a] |
|---|---|---|
| **Enhanced Student Learning**<br>Increased focus on outcomes<br>Increased focus on faculty productivity<br>Recognized need for graduates with skills in critical thinking, problem solving, and analysis | **Focus on Learning and Teaching**<br>Changing nature of outcomes assessment<br>Changing nature of teaching<br>Changing understanding of how students learn<br><br>Changing nature of students | **Student Learning** (VS)<br>**Assessment** (M)<br>Teaching methods<br>Holistic learning<br>Student development<br>Job preparation skills<br>At-risk students<br>**Involvement** (M)<br>Academic advising<br>First-year experience<br>Service learning<br>Faculty concerns |
| **Diversity**<br>Of students<br><br>Of institutions<br><br>Of perspectives | **Improve Access and Success for Diverse Students**<br>Factors affecting access and educational success<br><br>Educational benefits of diverse campus environments | **Multiculturalism and Diversity (VS)**<br>Meeting the needs of diverse subgroups (especially lesbian, gay, bisexual, and transgendered students; students with disabilities; students of color)<br>Creating inclusive communities<br>Programming<br>Training |
| **The Engaged Institution**<br>With communities<br>With economic development<br>With civic renewal | **Collaborations and Partnerships**<br>External (business, social service agencies, municipal, state, and federal governments)<br><br>Internal<br>External (other education institutions)<br><br>**Changing Government Roles** | **Collaboration** (S)<br>With community<br><br><br>Interdepartmental, with faculty<br>Between colleges |

| Higher Education and Societal Trends | American College Personnel Association Trends | Student Affairs Discourse Topics[a] |
|---|---|---|
| **Technology** | **Technology** | **Technology** (S) |
| Increase in distance learning | Growth of distance education | Distance learning |
| | In the classroom | In the classroom |
| | Out of the classroom | |
| | For administrative and support services | In the workplace |
| | Impossibility of keeping up | |
| **Restructuring and Institutional Transformation** | **Changing Nature of Work** | **Leadership** (S) |
| | Faculty roles | |
| Increase in part-time faculty | Adaptable workforce | Change in organizational structure |
| Increase in distance learning | Technology | **Technology** (M) |
| | Collaboration | **Collaboration** (S) |
| | Change in view of educators | |
| | Financial pressures | **Funding** (W), **Financial Aid** (W) |
| | Employee diversity | |
| | Valuing employees | Changing nature of leadership |
| **Accountability** | **Accountability** | **Social Issues** (S) |
| | Student behavior | **Funding** (W) |
| Learning productivity and outcomes assessment | Cost-efficiency | **Assessment** (M), **Retention** (M) |
| | Program effectiveness | |
| **Rising Costs and Shifting Funding Sources** | **Responding to the Rising Cost of Higher Education** | |
| **Globalization** | | **International Education** (W) |
| **Market Responsiveness** | | |
| Influence of student demands | | |
| Integration of higher education and the marketplace | | |
| Community college strong ties | | |
| Increase in for-profit higher education | | |

**Table 2.1** (*continued*)

| Higher Education and Societal Trends | American College Personnel Association Trends | Student Affairs Discourse Topics[a] |
|---|---|---|
| **Knowledge as Capital**<br>Information, knowledge, and wisdom becoming the new capital in a service-based, technologically enhanced economy<br>Lifelong learning | | **Student Affairs** (S)<br>Professional development<br>Professional organizations<br><br>**Social Issues** (S)<br>Alcohol and drugs<br>Gambling<br>Violence<br>Eating disorders<br>Suicide<br>Sexual and physical assault<br>Campus social environment<br>Discipline and judicial<br>**Greeks** (W) |

[a]Categories are rated: VS = very strong; S = strong; M = moderate; W = weak.

*Source:* For American College Personnel Association Trends (column two), data from Johnson and Cheatham, 1999.

affairs in academic units) have to offer. In this volume, we also assert the need to focus on the diversity of perspective, that is, recognizing that there are varying experience and knowledge bases from which we draw in academe. For example, some student affairs professionals' core preparation is in counseling, whereas others have their training in management and administration. Both are important to the success of student affairs organizations. In their appropriate focus on programming, training, and meeting the needs of a diverse student body, student affairs professionals need to be aware of this diversity of intellectual perspective.

Student affairs professionals also must realize that they live and work in a society that appears to be losing the imperative to address issues of access and equity. So although the values of access and equity continue to drive student affairs, these values are weakening in our society as a whole. Affirmative action is the current issue of controversy related to multiculturalism and diversity. Edgerton (1999) argues that there were three prevailing beliefs in the 1960s that gave momentum to a focus on access to higher education.

One was a belief that an investment in higher education reaped benefits not only for individuals but also for the nation at large. Another was a belief that government had a major role to play in our national life. A third was a gathering belief in a commitment to civil rights. Today all three of these beliefs are being questioned. The political discourse about investments in higher education has shifted to emphasize the benefits to individuals, both political parties are trying to reduce the role of government, and affirmative action is now under assault. At the federal level, President Clinton's position to "mend not end" affirmative action remains under attack. Student affairs professionals must consider how they will respond to and address the field's overarching values and principles related to equity and access in the coming post–affirmative action world.

**The Engaged Institution.** Our focus in this section, as outlined in the first chapter, is primarily on the need for institutions, specifically student affairs professionals and departments, to engage externally. Higher education institutions (especially research institutions and community colleges) increasingly are engaged in multiple ways with multiple communities. Some of this is due to the continued encroachment and intermingling of external constituencies with institutions and their processes (Penney, 1996). Other examples of engagement include college-business partnerships (Winston, 1999; Zemsky and Massy, 1995) and partnerships with other levels of education, especially K–12 (Haycock, 1996; Rhodes, 1999).

The need for and current focus on internal collaboration and partnerships are highlighted in both the ACPA Senior Scholars trends document and in the discourse of the field. The ACPA trends document also recognizes the importance of external partnerships, both educational and noneducational. However, within the discourse of the field, the evidence indicates that the only institutions significantly focusing on external relationships are the community colleges (and to a lesser degree research institutions), which have as an important aspect of their mission responding to the needs of their community. It is true that some aspects of student affairs work (for example, service learning, community service, and cooperative programs) are rooted in community engagement. However, all student affairs professionals, leaders, and departments at four-year institutions need to be more connected to the world beyond their institutional boundaries. This is an aspect of seeing the big picture. It is for the reason of external relationships that we also include the ACPA trend of changing government roles as congruent with the notion of an engaged institution. Student affairs professionals also must be cognizant of the workings of government and government-related policymaking organizations that influence their work. Any notion of being aware of and interacting with policymakers has been absent in the discourse of student affairs.

Most of the core principles of the field are internally focused. However, the notion that higher education in general and student affairs in particular have roles in assisting in transforming our society into a learning society speaks to engagement beyond institutional boundaries.

**Technology.** All three lists recognize the importance, the proliferation, and the continuing integration of technology in our work in student affairs. This force is impossible to ignore. However, in the analysis of issues currently being addressed by student affairs professionals, distance learning is still a minor topic. Apparently, few frontline student affairs professionals see distance learning as an issue that has much to do with them or with their responsibilities. This is a very dangerous mind-set to have because it means that student affairs professionals are probably not engaging in the discussions and planning related to distance learning that are occurring on most campuses right now. The Association of Governing Boards asserts that the new technologies and distance-learning endeavors are making state boundaries increasingly irrelevant (Rhodes, 1999). They describe the *learning anytime anywhere partnerships* that are intended to stimulate innovation and experimentation in distance-learning opportunities by traditional and new institutions. Distance learning will have an influence on all aspects of student affairs, not just financial aid and registration. The notion of distance learning certainly is related to the belief that learning occurs in diverse places and in diverse ways, so student affairs professionals need to challenge their own definitions of *places* and *ways* and view distance learning as an emerging aspect of their work.

**Restructuring and Institutional Transformation.** This trend, identified in Chapter One, appears to relate somewhat to the changing nature of work described in the ACPA document. It also was indirectly evidenced in the discourse of the field. Although there was no overall category in the discourse that could be labeled restructuring and institutional transformation or changing nature of work, some of the categories could match some of the subcategories identified by the ACPA document (that is, technology, collaboration, funding, and financial aid). In addition, the category of leadership in the discourse analysis had a focus on change and transformation (that is, the changing nature of leadership and changes in organizational structure); therefore it appears to match the spirit of the trend labeled restructuring and institutional transformation and is matched in the table with the overall trend. If there is any element missing from the discourse of the field in this category, it is the notion of the changes facing faculty. However, there was evidence in the discourse data of a focus on faculty in the student learning category as well as in the collaboration category. In a manner of speaking, this entire volume is about restructuring and institutional transformation for student affairs professionals. However, Chapters Five, Six, Seven, and Eight focus more specifically on the changes facing student affairs professionals and on recommendations for how practice could be shaped to address these changes.

**Accountability.** Under the trend of accountability, the ACPA Senior Scholars trends document identifies the issues of student behavior, cost-efficiency, and program effectiveness. Even though there was no category of accountability identified in the discourse of the field, some of the categories and subcategories appear to be related. For example, many of the social issues identified in the discourse of the field have to do with student behavior (for example, alcohol and drugs, gambling, violence, eating disorders, sexual and physical assault). Three subcategories in the discourse analysis also may be related. They are outcomes assessment and retention, both related to program effectiveness, and funding, which is related to cost-efficiency. However, the concern is that other than social issues, these are all relatively minor topics in the discourse of student affairs. Using the assessment of learning outcomes to shape practice is something student affairs professionals and departments must have as a focus as we enter this new century. Although this is addressed more specifically in Chapter Seven, it appears that the core principles of student affairs are related to this trend in two ways. First, the content of the discourse addresses issues related to students and their well-being and development, which is certainly addressed in the core principles. Second, in order to operationalize our core principles we must be held accountable for our actions: we must be able to provide evidence that we are meeting the needs of students.

**Rising Cost of Higher Education and Shifting Funding Sources.** Two trends in student affairs reflect the influence of this greater trend. The first is the move to cost center budgeting, especially in the development of auxiliary units, wherein a department or program (for example, residence halls) must generate in revenue what it intends to spend. In other words, units must be self-supporting. Another student affairs trend is the increase in privatization and outsourcing taking place on more and more campuses. Beyond the traditional areas that have been privatized (such as housekeeping and custodial services, police and security, bookstores, and food service and campus dining), health centers, counseling services, and residence halls have been added. An issue for student affairs professionals to consider is how the increase in privatization affects the ability of the department and the division to address the enduring values and principles identified previously. It might be assumed that the management company contracting to run a residence hall system will be much more interested in preserving the bottom line than in ensuring that its staff is working to enhance student learning and student development. This issue is addressed in more depth in Chapter Six.

**Globalization.** Trends in globalization, the growing influence of the marketplace, and the concept of the engaged institution most clearly require student affairs professionals to see the bigger picture. Globalization demands that individuals see the United States and its system of higher education as existing in the greater context of the world. It means seeing that what is happening in the world today influences what happens in American higher education, and vice versa. Recognizing the growing influence of the marketplace requires seeing that the longtime differentiations and distinctions between education and business, nonprofit and for-profit, and clients and customers are lessening, if not disintegrating. Being an engaged student affairs professional at an engaged institution means redefining one's role, one's constituencies, and one's goals. The concern here is that, as we indicated in a previous heresy, student affairs professionals tend not to look at the big picture. Evidence in both the ACPA trends and in the discourse analysis indicate that this heresy is true.

On a continuum ranging from proximate to distant, perhaps globalization and the internationalization of higher education is the most distant of the trends from the everyday experiences of student affairs professionals, save those working in study abroad programs and offices of international student affairs. However, the graduates of American higher education will be living in an increasingly international world. Student affairs professionals need to be a part of preparing students for that inevitability. It is therefore most surprising to us that the ACPA Senior Scholar trends document fails to mention globalization as a focus for research or practice. We have to believe that this is an oversight and not evidence of the conclusion that either globalization is not happening or that it is not important to student affairs. In fact, the National Association of Student Personnel Administrators (NASPA) is coordinating exchanges with France, the United Kingdom, Australia and New Zealand, Mexico, Germany, and Spain, while exploring possible exchanges with China and South Africa ("National Association of Student Personnel Administrators Exchange Team . . .," 2000). In the discourse, international education was a weak category. Student affairs professionals must realize that international boundaries are disintegrating in higher education. In fact, it is vital that we consider what globalization means for all aspects of student affairs.

**Market Responsiveness.** Student affairs divisions at traditional four-year institutions are not engaged adequately with the multiplicity of marketplaces in which they exist or are in some way connected. For example, for-profit higher education, closely linked with distance education, is a topic that is not being addressed by the student affairs profession (Love and others, 2000). An implication of this trend is that student affairs must be more engaged with the marketplace in all of its multiple forms. In fact, with the explosion of for-profit higher education, traditional higher education institutions find themselves in the very center of a roiling market. The National Education Association (1999) indicates in its report addressing market-driven and quality-driven futures that community colleges are most suited to survival in this new educational world. Most already have outreach centers in the community, large numbers of part-time and temporary faculty, and thriving distance education programs. Student affairs divisions at baccalaureate degree–granting institutions would do well to partner with and learn from their community college peers.

**Knowledge as Capital.** Perhaps this notion of the growing importance of higher education is taken for granted by the authors of the ACPA trends document and by most student affairs professionals. We saw little evidence that the field of student affairs was engaged in dialogue about or reflection on the ideas that our society is undergoing a significant transition whereby having a degree and knowledge is no longer enough "capital" to guarantee our success. In addition, students must be able to understand and apply knowledge in multiple contexts; in other words, they must exhibit wisdom. We found little discussion of lifelong learning, yet the notion that learning transcends knowledge acquisition is certainly implied in the list of core principles. This topic is addressed in more depth in Chapter Four.

**Student Affairs and Social Issues.** Finally, these two topics, student affairs and social issues, were identified as categories in the discourse analysis but not identified in either of the other sources. They are therefore not addressed in this volume. However, the solid appearance of these two strong categories in the discourse of the field provides, in a way, substantiation of the discourse analysis process and findings because they represent topics that have been and will probably always be issues of importance in the discourse of student affairs. It makes sense that they are important issues in student affairs yet would not be part of any trend analysis, because the topic of student affairs focuses on issues related to professional development and professional organizations, and the category of social issues focuses on a variety of student-related issues. However, even though student affairs professionals have dealt and always will deal with social issues, the particular social issues addressed at any one point in time will change. For example, issues of gambling on college campuses probably were not the focus ten years ago that they are today; conversely, suicide and alcohol and drugs are longtime issues of focus and promise to be for many years to come.

## Implications and Advice for Practice

We provide the following implications to assist with the process of discovering how these trends might influence student affairs work in the near future.

**Individual and Organizational Reflection.** One of the first implications emerging from this information is the necessity of student affairs professionals and student affairs departments to undergo a period of reflection, assessment, and planning. The following questions can help shape that process:

What evidence exists or is identifiable that you or your department operates from the perspective that the myths and assumptions we identified are true and accurate?

What insights can you gain for yourself or your department by playing "what if" with the heresies we identified?

To what degree are you and your department addressing the values and principles that continue to inform our profession?

To what degree are you and your department failing to address the trends that are currently occurring in our society and that are influencing higher education?

**Leading from Core Values.** In periods of transition and confusion, it becomes much more important for institutions consciously to discuss the core values and principles on which our work is based—or should be based. These principles can form a point of discussion around which it may be possible to build consensus as well as serve as an element of accountability when we ask of our actions and programs, How does this operationalize our core values and principles?

**Seeing the Big Picture.** In times of transition, the tendency is to focus inward. In fact, the previous implication is just such a suggestion—to focus inward on core values. However, at the same time, we must resist the urge to only focus inward, both individually and organizationally. To look inward, we must also look outward and beyond. We must be aware of the environmental changes and pressures occurring on our campus and must reach beyond our campus and become engaged with the multiple communities that exist beyond our borders, including governmental and policymaking bodies.

## Conclusion

Entering a new century is an exciting time for the student affairs profession. We are faced with unprecedented challenges and opportunities, as exhibited by the themes and trends that the first two chapters of this volume have described. We also enter this century with a set of core values and principles that should continue to guide our work now and in the future. However, we need to look beyond the traditional core values and seek others to guide us as well. We have proposed several and encourage readers to consider others. We also have pointed to societal and higher education trends and themes that do not appear to be addressed adequately by the profession. As a profession, we need to discover the gaps in our practice and to address them if we are to fulfill our mission of meeting the learning and developmental needs of our students.

## References

American College Personnel Association. *The Student Learning Imperative: Implications for Student Affairs.* Washington, D.C.: American College Personnel Association, 1994.

American Council on Education. *The Student Personnel Point of View.* Washington, D.C.: American Council on Education, 1937.

American Council on Education. *The Student Personnel Point of View.* Washington, D.C.: American Council on Education, 1949.

Arena, D., and Page, N. "The Imposter Syndrome in the Clinical Nurse Specialist Role." *Image,* 1992, *24*(2), 121–125.

Argyris, C. "Teaching Smart People How to Learn." *Harvard Business Review,* May–June 1991, pp. 99–109.

Bent, K. "Perspectives on Critical and Feminist Theory in Developing Nursing Praxis." *Journal of Professional Nursing,* 1993, *9*(5), 296–303.

Blimling, G. S., and Whitt, E. J. (eds.). *Good Practice in Student Affairs: Principles to Foster Student Learning.* San Francisco: Jossey-Bass, 1999.

Council of Student Personnel Associations in Higher Education. "Student Development Services in Post Secondary Education." *Journal of College Student Personnel,* 1975, *16,* 524–528.

Edgerton, R. "Education White Paper." Available on the Pew Charitable Trust Web site [http://www.pewtrusts.com]. Retrieved Sept. 2, 1999.

Haycock, K. "Thinking Differently About School Reform." *Change,* Jan.–Feb. 1996, *28,* 12–18.

Johnson, C. S., and Cheatham, H. E. (eds.). *Higher Education Trends for the Next Century: A Research Agenda for Student Success.* Washington, D.C.: American College Personnel Association, 1999.

Kuh, G. D., Bean, J. P., Bradley, R. K., and Coomes, M. D. "Contribution of Student Affairs Journals to the Literature on College Students." *Journal of College Student Personnel,* 1986, *27,* 292–304.

Love, P. G., and others. *A Discourse Analysis of the Student Affairs Profession: 1999–2000.* Unpublished manuscript, Kent, Ohio: Kent State University, 2000.

National Association of Student Personnel Administrators. *A Perspective on Student Affairs.* Washington, D.C.: National Association of Student Personnel Administrators, 1987.

"National Association of Student Personnel Administrators Exchange Team Sees Need for More International Visits." *National Association of Student Personnel Administrators Forum,* Mar.–Apr. 2000, *21*(4), 9.

National Education Association. "The Future of Higher Education: Market-Driven and Quality-Driven." [http://www.nea.org/he/future/market.html]. 1999.

Penney, S. "Five Challenges for Academic Leaders in the 21st Century." *Educational Record,* 1996, *77*(2–3), 19–22.

Rhodes, F. *Ten Public Policy Issues for Higher Education in 1999 and 2000.* Washington, D.C.: Association of Governing Boards of Universities and Colleges, 1999.

Roberts, S. "Oppressed Group Behavior: Implications for Nursing." *Advances in Nursing Science,* July 1983, *5*(4), 21–30.

Vaill, P. B. *Learning as a Way of Being: Strategies for Survival in a World of Permanent White Water.* San Francisco: Jossey-Bass, 1996.

Whelan, M. "Self-Esteem and Competitiveness Among Nurse Practitioner Students." Unpublished doctoral dissertation, Teacher's College, Columbia University, 1996.

Winston, G. C. "For-Profit Higher Education: Godzilla or Chicken Little?" *Change,* Jan.–Feb. 1999, *31*(1) 13–19.

Woolf, P. "Increasing Self-Esteem Through Self-Evaluation." *Journal of Nursing Education,* 1984, 23(2), 78–80.

Zemsky, R., and Massy, W. F. "Expanding Perimeters, Melting Cores, and Sticky Functions: Toward an Understanding of Our Current Predicaments." *Change,* Nov.–Dec. 1995, 27, 41–49.

3

*The changing nature of students in higher education and the implications of this diversification for student affairs professionals are discussed.*

# Students of the New Millennium

Throughout the 1980s and 1990s, literature has described the increasing diversification of the college student body. This chapter continues this pattern but also highlights some of the newer issues related to and facing college students as we enter a new century. The chapter has several purposes. The first is to explore some of the beliefs that appear to be operating in student affairs discourse about who our students are and what they want from their college experience. The second is to paint a picture of who our students are today as well as how the student population is changing. Our final purpose is to provide some implications of this information for student affairs professionals.

## Myths and Heresies

We argue that there is at least one heresy and several myths related to how student affairs professionals tend to view the college student population. The *heresy* is that *the field of student affairs continues to focus almost solely on the "traditional" undergraduate college student.* This heresy is based on the argument that much of our writing and discourse betrays an underlying and subconscious assumption that the typical college student is a traditional-age, full-time, middle-class undergraduate student living on campus or at home. For example, rarely do the writings on student learning (for example, Love and Love, 1995; Whitt, 1999) mention adult learners, the impact of part-time status on learning, the fact that 40 percent of students attend community colleges, the graduate student population, or the influence of social class on one's learning experience. The mainstream student affairs literature that does *not* betray these assumptions is focused on the topics of shifting student demographics (for example, El-Khawas, 1996; Kuh, 1990), is written in advocacy for special groups (for example, Fleming, 1984; Schlossberg, Lynch, and Chickering, 1989), or is produced by community college researchers and practitioners, who are acutely aware of the continuing changes in the college student population.

The core principles listed in Chapter Two focus heavily on our commitment to students. We must continually remind ourselves that this commitment is to *all* students. In fact, one of the *myths* related to the topic of changing college student populations is that *student affairs educators care about the experience of all students*. Care for all students is an enduring professional value and likely true, but some groups of students get far more of our attention than others. After half a century of touting changing student demographics, many campuses are still chilly climates for students of color, neglect adult learners and commuters, and act as if students in the "middle" need less attention than underprepared low-ability or talented high-ability students. Most traditional campuses have avoided exploring the needs of distance learners. We persist in thinking the word *student* really means *undergraduate* instead of all categories of students. In fact, we can state it as a *myth: graduate students do not have needs*. The graduate student population is the single most ignored block of students in relationship to services provided. The underlying assumptions related to graduate students include the belief that they are not in need of orientation to the institution, have no academic skill needs, have less need for individual academic advising, and do not need career advice or services. Student affairs professionals in general have not focused the kind of time and energy on the underrepresentation of students of color in the graduate population that they have on students of color in the undergraduate population. Even though women account for 56 percent of all graduate students, they are still a significant minority of students seeking first professional degrees (for example, law, medicine) (Hebel, 2000). The actual number of graduate and professional students enrolled at any one time is a bit difficult to determine. It is recognized that graduate and professional enrollment peaked in 1996, and despite declining slightly during the last several years, the enrollment of graduate and professional students is approximately two million ("The Nation," 1999), representing about 12 percent of the college-going population. Most student affairs professionals often ignore these students.

## Student Population Trends

We address two types of trends related to the college student population. The first is demographic trends. By this, we mean those changes in the college population related to how many and what types of students are going to college. The topics in this category should be of little surprise to anyone working in higher education as they have been reported on repeatedly and are updated here. These trends include information related to race, gender, age, increases in remedial education, and geographic shifts in attendance patterns. There are also those changes we refer to as developmental trends. These refer to changes occurring in the college student population that have to do with the experiences of the cohort of traditional-age students currently in college as well as those that we anticipate entering in the near future, because adolescents still constitute the single largest age block and present rapidly changing needs. These trends include the impact of societal changes that have resulted in adolescents' being left with a great deal of independence and lack of supervision, in changes in students' perceptions of society, in changes in patterns of student behaviors, and in the increased levels of emotional and psychological damage of entering students.

**Demographic Trends.** American higher education is in the midst of experiencing the effect of the baby boomlet, the children of baby boomers. After nearly fourteen years of declines, enrollments in primary schools began to experience annual increases starting in 1985. Those students approached college-going age in the late 1990s and are helping fuel a surge in college enrollments (Kellogg Commission on the Future of State and Land-Grant Universities, 1999). However, not all geographic areas and college student subgroups are experiencing the surge in the same way.

*Geographic Shifts.* Immigration and internal migration continue to reconfigure the higher education landscape. Despite overall increases in the college-going age group, some sections of the country, such as the Rust Belt (Chicago to Boston), can expect near zero growth in traditional-age college students. In fact, Massachusetts, Connecticut, New York, and Washington, D.C., are expected to see slight declines in the numbers of full-time college students (Dortch, 1997). At the same time, the student populations in the West, Southwest, and Southeast will continue to grow dramatically. In fact, higher education and governmental officials in California are discussing the need to add campuses to its state higher education system to handle the projected growth and anticipate opening a new campus in Merced by 2005 ("The Nation," 1999). Between 1997 and 2007, the student population attending college full-time will most likely grow from 9.8 million to 11.2 million (Dortch, 1997). Of that 1.4 million increase, almost half (about 540,000) will occur in three states (California, Texas, and Florida). Though their growth will be smaller in actual numbers, four states will probably see increases in full-time student growth of more than 30 percent in that same time period—Utah (50 percent), Alaska (37 percent), Nevada (33 percent), and Arizona (31 percent). In addition, Utah (26 percent), Nevada (19 percent), and Arizona (18 percent) expect to see significant increases in part-time enrollment (Dortch, 1997). These increases will most certainly put a strain on the higher education institutions in those states. It is important to note that these increases (especially the part-time population) are dependent in part on the status of the economy. If the economy during the first part of this decade continues to be strong, enrollment numbers may be less than stated here. However, if we experience a recession, enrollments may swell even further, because more people choose to continue in or return to school during economic downturns. This is especially the case for graduate enrollments, which have experienced slight declines during the last five years, due primarily to a robust economy (Schneider, 1998). An implication of this information is that student affairs professionals will have very different experiences depending on the location of their institution.

*Age.* There appear to be two differing perspectives on the future demography of adult students in higher education. One perspective sees the continuing dispersion of students across the age span. The other sees a shift in patterns related to those students over the age of twenty-five, due to the fact that higher percentages of people earn degrees while still in their early twenties, reducing future pools of adult undergraduates.

The first perspective continues to see increases in adult students and especially in those choosing to attend part-time or episodically. Edgerton (1999) points out that at this point fewer than one in six of all current undergraduate students fit the traditional stereotype of the American college student. Even those students who consider themselves to be attending full-time tend to remain in school longer. Bachelor's degrees should no longer be referred to as four-year degrees because fewer than 20 percent of entering college students will complete their degree in that time frame. More than half of all undergraduates are at least twenty-two years of age; almost a quarter are thirty years of age or older. The apparent implication of these statistics is that the adult college student population will continue to increase and to represent a greater and greater percentage of the total student body. However, because this population specifically will be targeted by nontraditional delivery systems (for example, Web-based courses, distance learning), competition for these students will likely be intense.

Somewhat counter to the "expansion" argument, Dortch (1997) asserts that due to a number of factors, enrollment patterns of non-traditional-age students are more difficult to predict than the enrollment patterns of the eighteen to twenty-five year olds. First, during the past several decades, as the baby boom generation's influence waned and the number of high school graduates declined, many institutions of higher education maintained enrollments by targeting older students who had not earned college degrees while in their twenties. As we enter this new century, the pool of adults without undergraduate degrees is shrinking; therefore an institution's ability to enhance undergraduate enrollments by targeting adult students may be limited. For these institutions, the appropriate market for adult students may be graduate education or certificate programs or other programs designed for lifelong learners who are seeking to update their credentials. One implication of this pattern that may surface during the next several decades is that traditional four-year institutions that expanded undergraduate enrollments with non-traditional-age students may revert back to the enrollment patterns of the 1960s and 1970s, when full-time student populations were almost totally of traditional age. If these institutions are interested in serving the needs of adult students, they will need to enhance their focus on advanced degree programs, postbaccalaureate certificate programs (Irby, 1999), life-long learning activities (Kellogg Commission on the Future of State and Land-Grant Universities, 1999), certificate programs, and specialized skill development. The latter two are specialties of community colleges.

*Gender.* The year 1979 marked the point in time when the attendance of women as a percentage of college students reached that of men. However, women did not stop working when they reached 50 percent of the student body. They have continued during the past two decades to constitute a larger and larger percentage of the college student population. In fact, much of the growth in the student population can be attributed to women. Between 1985 and 1995, the number of college women increased 23 percent, whereas men only increased 9 percent (Hansen, 1998). Today women have surpassed 55 percent of the student population and tend to graduate at higher rates than men. Despite the assertion that more jobs are requiring postsecondary education (King, 1999), there are economic drivers that may continue to exacerbate the gender disparity in college attendance. For example, with the proliferation and pervasiveness of technology, not only high-tech firms but also many other businesses requiring personnel with technological competence are finding it difficult to secure the number of college-educated employees they need. Perhaps this can open the door to technologically inclined high school graduates (still typically boys). It is difficult to say what implications this trend will have for higher education. Certainly, the issue warrants discussion and consideration.

*Race and Ethnicity.* Among the published themes that focus on the composition of our student body is the recognition that our student body will continue to become increasingly diverse throughout the first half of our new century (Eckel, Green, and Hill, 1997; Kuh, 1990). Edgerton (1999) points out, "As a consequence of both differential birth rates and of the 1965 immigration reform law, America's minorities are a rapidly growing segment of the total population. By 1990, minorities had increased to 20 percent of the total population. In the under-eighteen age group, this figure was 31 percent. Assuming that the average annual rate of increase in the minority population of children younger than eighteen continues at about 0.5 percent a year, soon after 2020, among citizens under age eighteen, 'minorities' will become the majority" (p. 19).

Although minorities are still not attending college at the rate of white students (Kellogg Commission on the Future of State and Land-Grant Universities, 1999), this shift in demographics in the population will continue to be seen in the increase of students of color attending institutions of higher education. Institutions, and the student affairs divisions within them, will continue to be faced with addressing and transforming chilly and unwelcoming environments for students of color, environments that create climates that are debilitating to the success of students of color (Steele, 2000).

**Developmental Trends.** Developmental trends refer specifically to those changes in the traditional-age population of students related to academics, identity development, and other issues of growth and maturation due especially to changing social contexts. Because many of these issues are due to shifting social and cultural contexts, they could also be issues for nontraditional students; however, the focus of this section is specifically on students of traditional age. Although a number of these trends may be considered negative and may provide significant challenges for higher education, there are a few trends that are positive. These developmental changes address another *myth* in student affairs, that *traditional students today are the same as traditional students of the past twenty or thirty years.* The information provided indicates that students are different in a number of ways, including levels of preparation, identity development, shifts in attitudes, and increased levels of psychological and emotional damage. The positive developments include higher levels of technological savvy, an increased focus on spirituality, and an increase in civic-mindedness.

*Preparedness.* A continuing trend that has been identified in the literature is that college students increasingly are underprepared (Hansen, 1998; Levine and Cureton, 1998) and need more help "catching up" in order to succeed in college. Seventy-three percent of college deans reported an increase in the last ten years of the proportion of students requiring remedial or developmental education (Levine and Cureton, 1998). According to a 1995 national survey by the U.S. Department of Education, slightly more than three-fourths of all colleges and universities offer remedial courses. Nearly one-third of all undergraduates reported having taken a basic skills or remedial course in reading, writing, or math (Levine and Cureton, 1998). In fact, 80 percent of all student work in mathematics courses in college is remedial. Even though some signs of improvement have been seen in high school (Hansen, 1998), this increase in remedial course work is expected to expand as we enter this new century, despite attempts by some systems of higher education to eliminate remedial education from the curriculum.

*Identity Development Issues.* As indicated previously, student affairs professionals seem to act under the assumption that although the population of college students may be changing in some demographically related ways, the traditional student has remained pretty much the same. This is a faulty assumption because the experiences of the population of students once considered of traditional age (that is, eighteen to twenty-two) are also changing. Hersch (1998) reports:

> Today's teens have grown up in the midst of enormous social changes that have shaped, reshaped, distorted, and sometimes decimated the basic parameters for healthy development. They have grown up with parents who are still seeking answers about what it means to be an adult man or woman. They have lived in families that seldom fit the old ideal of a family and in a culture where the traditional wisdom of how to raise children has been replaced by

a kind of daily improvisation as parents try to fit child rearing into their busy lives. At a time when adolescents need to emulate role models, the adults around them are moving targets [p.18].

Hersch also points out that for many middle-class adolescents there are no longer any clearly defined rites of passage—ways to find meaning and a prescribed place in the adult community—which are important identity development tasks. There is little meaning in getting a driver's license or turning eighteen for many of these teenagers, who have already assumed grown-up responsibilities for cooking, shopping, cleaning, self-care, and care of siblings. What may have been more the norm for students from working-class or working-poor backgrounds has now reached normality for many middle-class, suburban students. In addition, approximately 26 percent of freshmen in 1997 came from divorced families (Hansen, 1998), and 32 percent of all children lived in single-parent situations. This represents a threefold increase from 1972 (Hansen, 1998). Going beyond this information, it is clear that many of today's college students have lost more than secure families and adult interaction. They grow up in a world that lacks consistency and structure. They are frustrated that there are no magic formulas to attain financial security, job stability, or marital harmony. They are part of the first generation of college students who probably will not do as well economically as their parents. Technology and media create a world without boundaries. This makes these teenagers even more vulnerable than teenagers of the past.

The main problem for these emerging college students is the search for identity in this amorphous and unpredictable environment. Although it is an issue throughout the life span, identity development is the central task of the traditional college years, yet Hersch (1998) points out that the most stunning change for adolescents today is their aloneness. The adolescents of the nineties were more isolated and more unsupervised than those from other generations. Today both parents are at work, neighbors are often strangers, and relatives live in distant places. This changes everything. It changes access to a bed, a liquor cabinet, a car, and a gun, as tragedies in such places as Jonesboro, Arkansas, and Littleton, Colorado, clearly show. Younger and younger children have sole responsibility for making decisions in their lives, yet these decisions are often made in a void of aloneness.

*Shifts in Attitudes.* Like Hersch, Levine and Cureton (1998) point out that today's cohort of students lives in an era very different from that of previous generations of students. They point out that today's students believe that they are living in a deeply troubled nation where intractable problems are multiplying and solutions are growing more distant. They distrust the nation's political leaders. They have little confidence in the nation's social institutions (for example, churches and schools). They see large-scale problems all around them, from poverty, racism, and crime to environmental pollution and global conflict. Yet these students also feel that they do not have the luxury of turning away from the problems as the students in the 1980s—the "me generation"—could and did. They believe their generation has to fix everything. This generation of students does not expect government to come to the rescue. They have chosen instead to become involved in their community personally, in their neighborhood, and on their block. This may bode well for encouraging student involvement in building campus communities. In fact, this type of involvement is seen on campus in the increase in service activities among students.

Levine and Cureton also point out that we can expect to see clubs like the Young Democrats and Young Republicans continue to fade. In their place, ethnic, gender, and racially oriented support and advocacy groups have arisen and will continue to grow. These groups fulfill both social and political functions; therefore, as traditional political organizations are declining, campus activism will continue to climb. Levine and Cureton point out that in 1969, 28 percent of undergraduates reported having participated in a demonstration. That percentage plummeted in the 1970s and early 1980s. However, by the late 1990s, that number was back up to 25 percent and is predicted to climb as we enter this new century.

Diversity and multiculturalism continue to be stressful in the lives of our students and a source of tension on our campuses. Levine and Cureton found that the force of political correctness stifles conversation. They found that students were more willing to talk about the intimate details of their sex lives than about issues of race, ethnicity, and sexual orientation. Creating a climate on campus where issues related to difference can be explored, discussed, and worked through as a community will continue to be a challenge for student affairs professionals well into the new century.

*Increases in Psychological and Emotional Damage.* According to Hansen (1998), "While the overall number of violent crimes in society has gone down in recent years, violence among children and adolescents remains extremely high, despite some progress. A considerable percentage of students have grown up in an atmosphere of fear and intimidation that has carried from the streets into the schools. In addition, there is the particularly disturbing frequency of sexual assault on girls and young women" (p. 5).

Hansen goes on to point out that more than 25 percent of adult women report having been sexually assaulted during their childhood or as young women. Such students will arrive at college with emotional and psychological damage. Levine and Cureton (1998) substantiated that current students are more psychologically and emotionally damaged than students from previous years. The figures they report are staggering: sixty percent of the campuses they surveyed indicated record use of psychological services; eating disorders were up 58 percent in the last decade; drug abuse is up 42 percent; alcohol abuse is up 35 percent; and suicide attempts are up 23 percent.

Levine and Cureton discovered that this generation of college students fears intimacy in relationships more than past generations of students. So even though students are engaging politically, they are fearful of engaging interpersonally. Levine and Cureton point out that traditional dating is largely dead on college campuses, replaced by group dating, in which men and women travel in unpartnered groups. This behavior provides protection from deeper involvement and intimacy. Sex tends to be casual, without emotional attachment or commitment. Levine and Cureton found that students rationalized this type of social life by saying that they had never seen a successful adult romantic relationship. This assessment echoes what Hersch (1998) found in her study of adolescents: they are not around adults often enough to observe how they negotiate the tasks of adulthood.

*Positive Developments.* Levine and Cureton's work (1998) is used in the previous section to describe some of the more problematic trends in today's traditional-age college student population. However, as the word *hope* in the title of their book *(When Hope and Fear Collide)* implies, they also found positive developments in the lives of the college students they studied. These positive developments include increasing levels of civic engagement and activism, increasing levels of community service, and more hope and optimism related to their futures and to society in general.

In terms of adolescents, recent studies of teenagers also have revealed some changes in today's population that have positive elements and may bode well for their future. For example, Stevenson and Schneider (1999), in a study of more than seven thousand teens, found them to be more ambitious than previous generations of teens, though they also discovered that the teenagers needed more direction from adults, again reflecting the isolation identified by Hersch (1998). *New York Times*–CBS polls conducted with more than a thousand teens in 1994 and 1999 indicated additional positive changes in attitudes and perceptions. For example, the teens responding in 1999 reported fewer problems with violence, both at school and in the streets, than in 1994 and fewer worries. The percentage who said they feared being victimized dropped from 40 percent in 1994 to 24 percent in 1999, and those who believed it was harder for them to grow up than their parents dropped from 70 percent in 1994 to 43 percent in 1999 (Goldberg and Connelly, 1999). Other positive trends include increased technological savvy—from 45 percent reporting using a computer at home in 1994 to 63 percent in 1999 and almost 50 percent reporting that they regularly went on-line.

## Implications

Although the information on demographic trends warrants the attention and consideration of student affairs professionals, the trends related to developmental concerns on the whole represent sobering information. Although this information certainly sounds like a lot of bad news, it is important to recognize that every generation of college students arrives with its own particular challenges for student affairs professionals. One of the implications of this information for student affairs professionals is the need to challenge one's assumptions about who our students are, especially expanding beyond the traditional focus on undergraduates. Other implications are that there is and will continue to be a need for competent and energetic student affairs professionals who are trend watchers.

**Challenge Assumptions About Who You Think Your Students Are.** One of the core purposes of this volume is to challenge student affairs professionals to examine their assumptions and rework those that are discovered to be faulty. We have proposed heresies and identified myths. However, professionals need to examine their own assumptions as well. With regard to assumptions about students, it is possible that there may be a temptation to view the experiences of today's students and even tomorrow's students through the lens of our own experiences as college students earlier in the 1990s, the 1980s, or earlier still. If we were to do this, there would certainly be similarities, and we could very well then form a connection with the students of today and empathize with them, certainly an important thing to do. However, what would be missing from that consideration would be the differences between the experiences of those two groups of students. It is important to fully recognize that 2000 is not 1980 or 1990; it is not even 1996. Students today and those of the future face different challenges and have had different experiences than those of even a few years ago. The challenge is to see and to respond to those differences, while making appropriate and important connections through the similarities.

**Consider Graduate Students.** One assumption that warrants specific focus is the underlying notion that student affairs professionals serve the undergraduate population. Although NASPA has a network devoted to professionals working in academic administration and professional schools, graduate students are still routinely ignored by most of the student affairs profession. Pruitt-Logan and Isaac (1995) present one of the few attempts to address graduate student needs, but services have changed little. Undergraduates seem to be the domain of everyone, whereas graduate students are the responsibility of only their department, perhaps their program, and maybe only their adviser. This significant population of students needs to be a focus of discussion in the profession, including focusing on how their developmental and practical needs can be best met by institutions of higher education.

**Develop and Maintain Traditional Competencies.** Caring, competent, and reflective practitioners are needed in the student affairs profession—that is, professionals who reflect on and try to put into practice the principles noted in the previous chapter. We cannot count on our own experience and our past training to prepare us to meet the challenges of the future. What will be required is ongoing self-development and self-reflection. Among other requirements, this calls for extraordinary listening skills and a recognition that all students need to be listened to and learned from. It is important to listen for and discover how students' experiences vary from our own. These students need to be taught and encouraged to address any experiences that have stymied their development and to develop hope, responsibility, appreciation of differences, and personal efficacy and self-worth. This cannot happen only in the classroom; it must also happen in the other life laboratories that exist throughout campus (for example, advising relationships, student organizations, residence halls).

**Differentiate Between Student Needs and Student Desires.** An important question for student affairs professionals to consider is this: What are the expectations of tomorrow's traditional-age undergraduate students as they arrive on a campus that is more closely supervised than their own home? As mentioned earlier in the chapter, traditional-age students come to college desperately needing guidance, structure, role modeling, wisdom, and traditions but not wanting them because they are used to being independent. In fact, they may actually want these things but may say and act otherwise, out of fear. *Duty to care* has replaced *in loco parentis* as an underlying responsibility of higher education professionals. Duty to care is a broad term that can cover all students and means that although we are not in the place of parents for our traditional-age students, we have the responsibility to provide for their developmental needs and to treat them as adults. It is unethical to allow students to drift in the breeze of unsupervised and unstructured experience. We need to care for them and to provide for them. We need therefore to provide structure, guidance, and role models. This includes creating and promulgating expectations for community members. It also includes holding students responsible for their performance as students and for their behavior as members of a community.

**Know Your Student Body: Become Trend Watchers.** Komives and Kincart (1999) encourage student affairs professionals to look beyond their experiences with individuals or groups of students and to look for and consider trends in the greater population and have those trends and aspects of their student body drive administrative action and planning. They recommend benchmarking student experience on campus through data collection. They recommend benchmarking student experience on campus through data collection, either quantitatively (for example, Cooperative Institutional Research Program, College Student Experience Questionnaire) or qualitatively (for example, focus groups or observations). This creates an institutionally centered database that can be used to track changes in the overall student body. They also recommend involving younger professionals and consulting with faculty and staff who observe new students, such as English composition instructors, admissions counselors, orientation advisers and instructors, hall directors, and high school guidance counselors. They suggest clipping and saving texts related to student experience (for example, student newspapers). They also encourage student affairs professionals to challenge their assumptions about their students and to be open to making new meaning about them.

## Conclusion

Just as higher education is experiencing a permanent state of change—Vaill's "permanent white water" (1996, p. xiv)—so must student affairs professionals consider their student body to be in a permanent state of change. Changes on campus, in individual students, and in the student body in general are driven by changes in the social, economic, and cultural contexts of American higher education. Many of the trends that are mentioned in the first two chapters are influencing the student body. For example, technology is driving distance education and is creating a huge cadre of permanently off-campus students, and globalization is bringing the world to the campus and exposing the campus to more of the world. Student affairs professionals continually must consider how the core values and principles of the field drive their relationships with and service to their ever changing student population.

## References

Dortch, S. "A New Generation at College." *American Demographics* [http://www. demographics.com /publications/ad/97_ad]. Oct. 1997.

Eckel, P., Green, M., and Hill, B. *Transformational Change: Defining a Journey.* Washington, D.C.: American Council on Education, 1997.

Edgerton, R. "Education White Paper." Available on the Pew Charitable Trust Web site [http://www.pewtrusts.com]. Retrieved Sept. 2, 1999.

El-Khawas, E. "Student Diversity on Today's Campuses." In S. R. Komives and D. B. Woodard, Jr. (eds.), *Student Services: A Handbook for the Profession.* (3rd ed.) San Francisco: Jossey-Bass, 1996.

Fleming, J. *Blacks in College: A Comparative Study of Students' Success in Black and White Institutions.* San Francisco: Jossey-Bass, 1984.

Goldberg, C., and Connelly, M. "Fear and Violence Declined Among Teen-Agers, Poll Shows." *New York Times* [http://www.nytimes.com/library/national/102099violence _poll_edu.html]. Oct. 20, 1999.

Hansen, E. J. "Essential Demographics of Today's College Students." *American Association for Higher Education Bulletin,* 1998, *51*(3), 3–5.

Hebel, S. "Women Gain on Men in Attending College, Study Finds." *Chronicle of Higher Education* [http://www.chronicle.com/weekly/v46/i35/35a03802.htm]. May 5, 2000.

Hersch, P. *A Tribe Apart: A Journey into the Heart of American Adolescence.* New York: Fawcett Columbine, 1998.

Irby, A. J. "Postbaccalaureate Certificates: Higher Education's Growth Market." *Change,* 1999, *31*(2), 36–41.

Kellogg Commission on the Future of State and Land-Grant Universities. *Returning to Our Roots: The Engaged Institution.* Washington, D.C.: National Association of State Universities and Land-Grant Colleges, 1999.

King, P. "Improving Access and Educational Success for Diverse Students: Steady Progress but Enduring Problems." In C. S. Johnson and H. E. Cheatham (eds.), *Higher Education Trends for the Next Century: A Research Agenda for Student Success.* Washington, D.C.: American College Personnel Association, 1999.

Komives, S. R., and Kincart, J. B. "Innovative Methods for Understanding the Millennial Generation." Paper presented at the annual conference of the National Association of Student Personnel Administrators, New Orleans, March 29, 1999.

Kuh, G. D. "The Demographic Juggernaut." In M. J. Barr and M. L. Upcraft (eds.), *New Futures for Student Affairs: Building a Vision for Professional Leadership and Practice.* San Francisco: Jossey-Bass, 1990.

Levine, A., and Cureton, J. S. *When Hope and Fear Collide: A Portrait of Today's College Students.* San Francisco: Jossey-Bass, 1998.

Love, P. G., and Love, A. G. *Enhancing Student Learning: Intellectual, Social, and Emotional Integration.* ASHE-ERIC Higher Education Report no. 4. Washington, D.C.: School of Education and Human Development, George Washington University, 1995.

Pruitt-Logan, A. S., and Isaac, P. D. *Student Services for the Changing Graduate Student Populations.* San Francisco: Jossey-Bass, 1995.

Schlossberg, N. K., Lynch, A. Q., and Chickering, A. W. *Improving Higher Education Environments for Adults: Responsive Programs and Services from Entry to Departure.* San Francisco: Jossey-Bass, 1989.

Schneider, A. "Enrollments Fall Again at Graduate Schools, Report Says." *Chronicle of Higher Education* [chronicle.com/weekly/v45/i16/16a02001.htm]. Dec. 11, 1998.

Steele, C. M. "'Stereotype Threat' and Black College Students." *About Campus,* 2000, 5(2), 2–4.

Stevenson, D., and Schneider, B. *The Ambitious Generation: America's Teenagers, Motivated but Directionless.* New Haven, Conn.: Yale University Press, 1999.

"The Nation." *Chronicle of Higher Education Almanac,* 1999, p. 7.

Vaill, P. B. *Learning as a Way of Being: Strategies for Survival in a World of Permanent White Water.* San Francisco: Jossey-Bass, 1996.

Whitt, E. J. *Student Learning as Student Affairs Work: Responding to Our Imperative.* Washington, D.C.: National Association of Student Personnel Administrators, 1999.

4

*Changes in learning and development and the role that student affairs professionals must play in creating and sustaining learning and developmental communities are explored in this chapter.*

# Learning and Development

Chittister's commentary on the Rule of St. Benedict notes that "Benedict teaches life is a learning process. Western culture and its emphasis on academic degrees, however, has almost smothered this truth. . . . We have made the words 'graduation' and 'education' almost synonymous. We measure achievement in academic credits. We discount experience, depth, and failure. . . . All of that kind of achievement is nothing but a spiritual wasteland if along the way we have not attached ourselves to the discovery of truth, the cultivation of beauty, and the recognition of the real learnings of life" (cited in Vaill, 1996, p. 191).

The focus of today's colleges and universities grew out of the 1960s and 1970s cry for relevance. Going to college began to be viewed less as a rite of passage than it had been in previous generations and to millions of students came to be viewed more as an instrument for acquiring new careers and new ways of knowing. By pushing and pulling around the edges, college students largely reshaped the focus of the curriculum by asking, How can I use this? and How does this apply to my career plans? Even the most resistant disciplines have somewhat repackaged their content to demonstrate clear links to application and practical context. Challenges to the relevance of the Western canon transformed general education requirements to include more diverse perspectives. Biology laboratories tackle ecological issues, and sociology classes do field studies in ethnically diverse neighborhoods with service learning credits. Contemporary lessons from studying Shakespeare are reinforced anew with Claire Danes playing Juliet to Leonardo Di Caprio's Romeo. Faculty who cling to a rationalistic perspective of developing only the head but neglecting the heart increasingly are perceived by students as "dinosaurs." The challenges of teaching and learning in today's times require educators to develop an instrumental or pragmatist perspective (Young,

1996). This new *instrumental humanism* moves beyond combining knowledge and experience (Lloyd-Jones, 1954) to expecting higher levels of understanding and wisdom facilitated by experience.

This chapter explores the myths, heresies, trends, and core values that influence views of teaching, learning, and personal development in higher education. Specific attention is devoted to how the shift in focus from teaching to learning may bring a hopeful transformation in reconnecting higher education to student outcomes.

## Myths and Heresies

It is useful to examine prevalent views held in higher education about teaching and learning to guide a movement to more student-centered practices. A central, prevailing *myth* is that *the primary educational role of college is to impart knowledge.* Perhaps that was once a truth, but embracing it today perpetuates a myth that knowledge alone is the apex of learning. The conceptualization of knowledge as capital supports the view that those who know how to organize chunks of information are of value as knowledge holders; in actuality, what is valued is their ability to be wise (that is, make meaning, understand, and know how to apply) with that knowledge. The outcomes of today's college experience must move beyond knowledge toward enhancing understanding and personal wisdom. Indeed the sequence may be that data→information→knowledge→understanding→wisdom→action.

This movement recognizes the transforming process of learning and development through which massive amounts of data need to become useful information; information needs to become knowledge; knowledge needs to become real through understanding; understanding leads to wisdom; and wisdom leads to heightened capacity for being and doing. Versions of this model have informed educators for centuries. Educational systems (including higher education) have done remarkably well leading to the knowledge stages of this model. The "sage-on-the-stage" methods of teaching, Internet-based information systems, the concept of distribution requirements, majors, and even the structural organization into academic departments all support ways of sifting through massive amounts of data to seek meaning so that it becomes useful information that can be organized and transmitted (for example, taught) as knowledge. We reach knowledge transmission just fine; we have become very good at that. But it is insufficient as an outcome for today's learners. The primary educational role needs to be building the capacity for wisdom.

Another myth that blocks educational impact is the *myth* that *learning and personal development are separate processes.* It is simplistic to think that the curriculum is the realm of learning, and the co-curriculum is the realm of personal development. Learning and development are integrated, symbiotic processes. The most seamless elements in the college setting are the students themselves. Students take their heads and their hearts everywhere they go. They know that learning is inherently developmental and that personal development is a learning process. Significant college outcomes, like civic responsibility, can be accomplished only when head and heart are joined in commitment to action. "Civic responsibility and productive citizenship require not only cognitive complexity but affective complexity and commitment as well" (Baxter Magolda and Terenzini, 1999, p. 21).

Lip service to diverse learning styles has led to little change in practice. Linguistic and logico-mathematical intelligences may have been central to institutions promoting information or knowledge acquisition outcomes, but they are insufficient to assess levels of understanding or skill in application. Too many classroom educators think that learning is all linguistic and logico-mathematical, and conversely too many student affairs educators profess to value experiential learning but have no intentionality about the learning aspect of experience. It is a *heresy* to admit that *higher education does not value multiple intelligences or diverse ways of learning.* It is highly likely that most faculty teach the way they like to learn (largely through abstract conceptualization), most counselors counsel in a style they like best, and most administrators seek order and control. This is understandable but must be challenged to transform pedagogy and policy to respond to diverse learners. Linguistic and logico-mathematical intelligences are far more valued than emotional, interpersonal, kinesthetic, or other forms of intelligence (Gardner, 1993; Goleman, 1995). Although it is wonderful that there is increased attention being given to learning, the next frontier is to redesign learning experiences to be reflective of diverse ways of learning.

An often unspoken *myth* is the assumption that *personal development is really a luxury—an outcome of select private residential colleges.* The developmentally powerful environment of the classic residential liberal arts college is undeniable, yet it is wrong to assume that only those characteristics and resources can promote student development. That is not the only way. At larger institutions, those working with commuters too often feel hopeless about truly having an impact on students' development. In truth, development happens everywhere, whether planned or not. Indeed "serendipity is too important to leave to chance" (Kuh, in press). The challenge is for diverse institutions to facilitate holistic development within their mission and resources. Designing learning experiences that integrate intellectual, social, and emotional elements enriches the development and learning for more students (Love and Love, 1995). Students learn good *and* bad things from their experiences. They learn that they can trust institutional agents or should avoid them, that they can learn from peers or not, and that learning is relevant to experience or separate from it. The planful integration of college resources directed at student learning and student development is an imperative for all institutions.

The transformation needed to embrace diverse approaches to learning and development is often thwarted by institutional practices. It is a *heresy* to admit that *higher education institutions do not function as learning organizations.* It is indeed a paradox that institutions of higher education, known for creating and advancing knowledge, do not themselves function as learning organizations. They do not have useful mechanisms for bringing new information into the practices that are challenged by changing times. Fragmentation keeps key groups from learning from one another, and the press for scholarly productivity keeps faculty from campus citizenship obligations. Campus politics and bureaucratic hierarchies often interfere with quality, improvement, and flexibility. Indeed we have few useful mechanisms for residence life staff to make suggestions to academic advisers, or for counseling center staff to suggest new strategies to orientation planners, or for sociology faculty to find their way into addressing a campus racial crisis.

## Themes and Trends

Some encouraging trends hold promise in moving higher education toward strategies and opportunities for truly developing understanding and wisdom that may help students leave as learners, not just as graduates.

The 1980s emphasis on teaching has broadened to signal a new trend with an emphasis on learning (Edgerton, 1999). In the 1980s and 1990s, some promoted the profession of college teaching by seeking to distinguish between teaching faculty and research faculty. Some institutions thrive in that distinction (teaching versus research institutions), yet in reality faculty at teaching institutions acknowledge that they must maintain a record of scholarship to have any chance at mobility in the broader higher education work system. The acknowledgment that faculty are trained to be discipline or content experts rather than to be teaching experts led to the concept of a doctorate in teaching as a new kind of degree. Yet this changed little. The many 1980s and 1990s calls for stronger teaching at research universities evolved to re-center faculty on the importance of their teaching role and were advanced by teaching awards, revised tenure policies including post-tenure review, and public accountability for engaging faculty with their undergraduates. This faculty-focused discussion on teaching led to the late 1990s and early 2000s focus on student learning. Identifying how students learn opens the discussion about how to connect pedagogy to the context and motivation of the learner and may lead to more complex learning outcomes for more learners.

Although higher education does not seem to value multiple intelligences, there is an encouraging trend evident in the emphasis on learning that has broadened traditional passive pedagogies to value and implement more active learning modes. Baxter Magolda (1999) observes, "Active learning necessitated new assumptions about learning, knowledge, students, educators, and student affairs practice. Viewing learning as the continual reconstruction of belief in the integration of personal experience and existing knowledge brings students to center stage as partners in learning. Educators take more responsibility for managing the process and less responsibility for controlling the content" (p. 43).

Active learning was well conceived by the American Association for Higher Education (AAHE) (1998) work on the *powerful pedagogies* of service learning, problem-based learning, collaborative learning, and experiential learning. Although asserting a trend toward active learning is a bit of a myth, at least there is a crack in the sage-on-the-stage paradigm and what we hope is a transforming trend. We could go a step further and ask, What changes will occur if we shift focus to help students succeed in the lives they are living instead of insisting that college be the focus of their lives?

Although there is still too much formal separation of in-class and out-of-class learning experiences, an exciting trend toward the recognition that learning happens everywhere is emerging. Campuses moving toward living-learning centers, integrated freshman studies programs, credit for service learning, and senior capstone experiences acknowledge that learning happens everywhere. "Structurally and functionally, the present boundaries [between academic and student affairs] must be blurred to reflect the *joint and synergistic* (italics in original) effects of students' in and out-of-class experiences on learning" (Baxter Magolda and Terenzini, 1999, p. 23). From integrating K–16 programs, to getting credit for off-campus work experiences, to blending the traditional curriculum and co-curriculum, faculty and academic planners are admonished on many fronts to promote seamless learning environments, aligning campus policies and practices with core values and principles. Technology has made synchronous and asynchronous distance learning possible, and Web-based delivery of information—of everything from courses, to résumé writing techniques, to exploring opportunities for campus activities involvement—brings information into students' lives in a just-in-time fashion not dependent on office hours. Learning happens everywhere.

## Enduring Principles and Transcendent Values

The focus on learning has opened an examination of the who, how, where, what, and why of learning. Even though higher education has to change many practices, there are some enduring principles of learning that can guide this transformation.

A basic tenet of the student affairs profession is the development of the whole person. Indeed an enduring value that student affairs educators bring to the current trends on teaching and learning is this value of holistic development. Different campus resources and missions mean that this holistic development may vary in emphasis, but the profession must continue to promote all possible ways for a college to connect all of the resources in a learner's life (for example, families, work, faith) to the formal learning offered (for example, classes, co-curricular experiences).

A solid principle is that learning is social and interactive. When the public library movement spread in the United States, doomsayers forecast the demise of the public school system. After all, if anyone could get books free from the library, what role could the schools possibly fulfill? As we begin a new century, we hear the same concern about the Internet and cyber-learning. After all, if anyone can take courses on the Web from home, why do we need campus-based, postsecondary education? Knowledge can be acquired in independent, individualistic endeavors, yet true wisdom is promoted in social, interactive settings. The powerful findings from years of research on students' experiences affirm the power of peer influences in learning and development (Astin, 1993).

The enduring value that each individual is unique leads to a new principle—that learning occurs best among diverse people in diverse places and in diverse ways. Hurtado, Milem, Clayton-Pedersen, and Allen (1999) document the benefits of diverse students in diverse learning environments. Such diversity influences essential outcomes, such as "improvements in students' ability to engage in more complex thinking about problems and to consider multiple perspectives, and improvements in intergroup relations and understanding" (p. v). Merely being in the same environment does not accomplish those outcomes, but intentional practices that engage diverse students in contact with one another does reduce prejudice and does relate to those outcomes.

In addition to principles and values from the student affairs field applied to learning and development, there are key principles about learning that should be applied to the transformation of learning in a particular context. The 1990s emphasis on student learning and development led leaders in organizing learning environments to ask what is known and understood about learning that can serve as grounding principles for conceptualizing the transformation of learning on campus. The *learning principles and collaborative action* presented in *Powerful Partnerships* (American Association for Higher Education, 1998) follow (italics in original):

- Learning is fundamentally about *making and maintaining connections:* biologically through neural networks; mentally among concepts, ideas, and meanings; and experientially through interaction between the mind and the environment, self and other, generality and context, deliberation and action [p. 5].
- Learning is enhanced by *taking place in* the context of a *compelling situation* that balances challenge and opportunity, stimulating and utilizing the brain's ability to conceptualize quickly and its capacity and need for contemplation and reflection upon experiences [p. 7.]
- Learning is an *active search for meaning* by the learner—constructing knowledge rather than passively receiving it, shaping as well as being shaped by experiences [p. 8].
- Learning is *developmental,* a cumulative process *involving the whole person,* relating past and present, integrating the new with the old, starting from but transcending personal concerns and interests [p. 10].

- Learning is done by *individuals* who are intrinsically *tied to others as social beings,* interacting as competitors or collaborators, constraining or supporting the learning process, and able to enhance learning through cooperation and sharing [p. 11].
- Learning is strongly *affected by the educational climate* in which it takes place: the settings and surroundings, the influences of others, and the values accorded to the life of the mind and to learning achievements [p. 13].
- Learning requires *frequent feedback* if it is to be sustained, *practice* if it is to be nourished, and *opportunities to use* what has been learned [p. 15].
- Much learning *takes place informally and incidentally,* beyond explicit teaching or the classroom, in casual contacts with faculty and staff, peers, campus life, active social and community involvements, and unplanned but fertile and complex situations [p. 17].
- Learning is *grounded in particular contexts and individual experiences,* requiring effort to transfer specific knowledge and skills to other circumstances or to more general understandings and to unlearn personal views and approaches when confronted by new information [p. 18].
- Learning involves *the ability of individuals to monitor their own learning,* to understand how knowledge is acquired, to develop strategies for learning based on discerning their capacities and limitations, and to be aware of their own ways of knowing in approaching new bodies of knowledge and disciplinary frameworks [p. 20].

## Challenges to Learning and Development

The next decade will require that educators address these new learning challenges. We think it would be useful to the momentum on promoting a learning agenda to consider these areas of emphasis.

**Acknowledge That Workforce Demands Are Changing.** New workforce demands require a shift from the systems of a traditional education to those of a new workplace (American Council on Education, 1999). The educational experiences needed to produce those outcomes in students are profoundly different than those addressed by traditional educational practices (see Table 4.1).

**Focus on How to Teach for Understanding.** The responsibility of the teacher-school-education system has been focused around delivering knowledge, assessing how much is learned, and credentialing learning through course credits, hours, and grades. Sadly, little attention has been devoted to the stages of transforming knowledge through understanding into personal wisdom that can inform individual (and collective) thought and action. Understanding requires the active engagement of the learner with the material. The powerful pedagogies movement of the 1990s focused attention on just that process (American Association for Higher Education, 1998). Even though active learning strategies have been known for years (for example,

**Table 4.1. Mismatch Between Education and the Workplace**

| Traditional Education | Workplace Requirements |
|---|---|
| Facts | Problem solving |
| Individual effort | Team skills |
| Passing a test | Learning how to learn |
| Achieving a grade | Continual improvement |
| Individual courses | Interdisciplinary knowledge |
| Receiving information | Interacting and processing information |
| Technology separate from learning | Technology integral to learning |

Source: Data from American Council on Education, 1999.

Dewey, Kolb), the most systematic use of them for credit in college has been in laboratory instruction in the sciences and to some degree in discussion sections in lecture courses. The current emphasis on service learning, leadership development, capstone immersion experiences, internships, collaborative learning, consultation projects, and reflective activities like journaling are encouraging because they show movement in transforming the formal curriculum by using, and therefore expecting, more active pedagogies.

**Develop and Promote a Student Affairs Learning Agenda.** Student affairs staff also must examine our own practices to facilitate understanding and wisdom. Things that happen to students do not become "experience" without reflection. Despite all the rhetoric of Dewey's teachable moments, many practitioners—group advisers, counselors, or administrators—do not engage with students to ask the Kolbian reflective questions, What meaning do we make from this? What have we learned from this? How might this shape what you think or would do next time? In addition, student affairs staff often do not challenge students to apply their course-based or other formal learning to their co-curricular experience. Too few student government advisers ask, What do you know from sociology or political science that would help us understand what is going on here? How can you apply the freshman orientation reading to what just happened? or What information or skills do we need to address this new opportunity? Helping students mine the learning out of their experience is a powerful example of teaching them to be lifelong learners. The challenge to student affairs professionals is to engage as learners themselves by reading freshman orientation books and by connecting disciplinary knowledge bases with these real problems. Student affairs staff have to know more about their students—their majors, career goals, course work—and to engage the context of the students' experience with their co-curricular learning.

**Examine How Higher Education Credentials Learning.** Conventional ways to credential learning revolve around the Carnegie unit of time spent in class contact, evaluated by letter grades. Former AAHE president and director of Pew Charitable Trusts Russell Edgerton asks how we might evaluate learning differently. This change may be more than a few decades in the making, but the questions need to be asked now. A step toward this new kind of credentialing may exist now in the growing number of certificate programs that require combinations of courses, service, reflection, and other experiences. Portfolios and developmental transcripts deserve more of our attention; however, how to evaluate that mix is indeed a challenge.

**Get Serious About Outcomes Assessment.** Calls for assessment have existed since the founding of the profession and by the end of the 1990s became a cacophony of pleas to assess everything—needs, outcomes, program evaluation. The calls for assessment come from legislators, parents, funding and accrediting agencies, and students themselves. The most systematic assessment that colleges can muster are the credits and grades earned. We need to move beyond knowledge outcomes to assessing process outcomes like critical thinking and social responsibility (Baxter Magolda and Terenzini, 1999). Sadly, student affairs has not risen to this challenge. We desperately need to inculcate a culture of "systematic inquiry" into professional practice (Pascarella and Whitt, 1999, p. 91).

**Rise to the Challenge of Creating a Nation of Learners.** The wise leaders at Wingspread who challenged American higher education in the early 1990s to look again at what America expects from higher education concluded that America needs an educational system that takes values seriously, that focuses on learning, and that helps create a "nation of learners" by promoting lifelong learning (Wingspread Group on Higher Education, 1993, p. 7). This is still a timely challenge, and higher education has not yet seriously reconstructed the outcomes of college lifelong learning instead of producing just graduates. One outcome of the retention movement of the last thirty years has been a focus on persistence to graduation. In *Learning as a Way of Being,* Vaill (1996) comments about higher education that sadly, "There is no mission to produce learners. The mission is to produce graduates, as measured by some fixed amount of information correctly regurgitated on examinations and term papers" (p. 191). Conceptualizing our mission as producing lifelong learners will require new systems and new outcome measures. These new systems and measures must be adaptive to rapidly changing information about different pedagogies focused on teaching how to learn, as opposed to those pedagogies currently employed that focus both on teaching and acquisition of knowledge. A shift in our mission focus to producing lifelong learners might also bring with it new obligations for offering continuing education to alumni. Given their missions and past performance, institutions like community colleges have the most potential to educate a nation of learners, but all institutions need to reconstruct their educational role to consider the ongoing education of all citizens.

## Implications and Advice for Practice

What are the ways in which student affairs professionals can provide leadership in an area that too frequently has been considered "out of bounds" by us and by others? How can we work with our faculty colleagues to confront the myths of learning that inhibit the development of our students, our institutions, and ourselves as professionals? The following paragraphs offer some advice for practice that will help in the transformation of our communities into powerful places of learning and development.

**Be Scholar-Practitioners.** Professional practice requires action grounded in the scholarship of the student experience in higher education. Research, assessment, and evaluation must be applied systematically to professional practice. Systematic inquiry has to become a rewarded expectation of professionals. Policy and practice based in foundational theoretical and conceptual scholarship and informed by research, assessment, and evaluation is essential.

**Become a True Learning Organization.** Modeling is one of the most powerful learning modes. Students who see professionals reflecting on failure and mistakes, growing, learning, and facing shared challenges in productive ways will learn to do that themselves. Just how do the staff, faculty, and campus learn together? Aligning our organizations around our core pervasive value of learning is essential. We must shake loose our expectations that we, or others, should be experts in all we do and embrace that together we have a shared knowledge that can be used to address complex organizational challenges. This means getting comfortable with not knowing. Vaill says, "It is not an exaggeration to suggest that everyone's state of 'beginnerhood' is only going to deepen and intensify so that ten years from now each of us will be even more profoundly and thoroughly settled in the state of being a perpetual beginner" (1996, p. 81). As we propose in Chapter Seven, learning together will be key to leading our organizations in these rapidly changing times.

**Create and Nurture a Student-Centered Philosophy on Campus.** The 1990s brought a new attention to students as the core work of higher education. This is well evidenced by the land grant colleges' examination of their historic mission and purpose and the publication of their first blue ribbon papers, *Returning to Our Roots: The Student Experience* (Kellogg Commission on the Future of State and Land-Grant Universities, 1997). Enhancing the experience for any group of students (for example, students of color, women) helps improve the experience for all students (Hurtado, Milem, Clayton-Pedersen, and Allen, 1999; Sadker and Sadker, 1988). Focusing on students helps all educators be open to new ways of practice and keeps institutions linked to their mission and values. Too many institutions profess to be student centered but never go beyond the false promise of a platitude, because the philosophy is not evidenced in practice. Practices guided by the needs of and promises to students are essential. They range from adequate customer service (for example, evening office hours) to sound educational planning (for example, scheduling sufficient foundational courses to meet demands for these prerequisites) to creative pedagogy (for example, examining the first-year student experience and planning cluster courses).

**Organize Learning Differently.** It will, admittedly, take years and years for higher education to change from the tradition of the Carnegie classification system. After all, we are still trying to establish articulation agreements to transfer credits among our institutions. We can, however, create new innovative structures to explore learning packages led by student affairs staff who combine the curriculum, co-curriculum, and off-campus life of students. We can establish certificate programs in student affairs that require course work, co-curricular experience, off-campus experiences (such as in work or service) and assess key credentials with portfolios, oral examinations, Web page development, or narrative supervisor or mentor assessments. We can try something like certificates in leadership, multicultural competence, mentoring, or wellness.

## Conclusion

An emphasis on learning and development is a student-centered focus. Anything and everything student affairs professionals do to keep the resources of the institution focused on the student experience is essential for transforming the institution into a student-centered learning environment. Each student affairs office should be able to map its learning and developmental agenda and should identify educational strategies that are useful in the context of work with students. It is essential that the institution move beyond the acquisition of knowledge to the use of powerful pedagogies that help the learner find true understanding and a measure of wisdom.

## References

American Association for Higher Education. *Powerful Partnerships: A Shared Responsibility for Learning.* Washington, D.C.: American Association for Higher Education, American College Personnel Association, and National Association of Student Personnel Administrators, 1998.

American Council on Education. *The Kellogg Forum on Higher Education Transformation.* Washington, D.C.: American Council on Education, 1999.

Astin, A. W. *What Matters in College: Four Critical Years Revisited.* San Francisco: Jossey-Bass, 1993.

Baxter Magolda, M. B. "Engaging Students in Active Learning." In G. S. Blimling and E. J. Whitt (eds.), *Good Practice in Student Affairs: Principles to Foster Student Learning.* San Francisco: Jossey-Bass, 1999.

Baxter Magolda, M. B., and Terenzini, P. T. "Learning and Teaching in the 21st Century: Trends and Implications for Practice." In C. S. Johnson and H. E. Cheatham (eds.), *Higher Education Trends for the Next Century: A Research Agenda for Student Success.* Washington, D.C.: American College Personnel Association, 1999.

Edgerton, R. "Education White Paper." Available on the Pew Charitable Trust Web site [http://www.pewtrusts.com]. Retrieved Sept. 2, 1999.

Gardner, H. *Multiple Intelligences: The Theory in Practice.* New York: Basic Books, 1993.

Goleman, D. *Emotional Intelligence.* New York: Bantam Books, 1995.

Hurtado, S., Milem, J. F., Clayton-Pedersen, A. R., and Allen, W. R. *Enacting Diverse Learning Environments: Improving the Campus Climate for Racial/Ethnic Diversity.*

ASHE-ERIC Higher Education Report no. 8. Washington, D.C.: George Washington University, 1999.

Kellogg Commission on the Future of State and Land-Grant Universities. *Returning to Our Roots: The Student Experience.* Washington, D.C.: National Association of State Universities and Land-Grant Colleges, 1997.

Kuh, G. D. "College Students Today: Why We Can't Leave Serendipity to Chance." In P. Altbach, P. Gumport, and B. Johnstone (eds.), *In Defense of the American University.* Baltimore: Johns Hopkins University Press, in press.

Lloyd-Jones, E. "Changing Concepts of Student Personnel Work." In E. Lloyd-Jones and M. R. Smith (eds.), *Student Personnel Work as Deeper Teaching.* New York: Harper-Collins, 1954.

Love, P. G., and Love, A. G. *Enhancing Student Learning: Intellectual, Social, and Emotional Integration.* ASHE-ERIC Higher Education Report no. 4. Washington, D.C.: School of Education and Human Development, George Washington University, 1995.

Pascarella, E. T., and Whitt, E. J. "Using Systematic Inquiry to Improve Practice." In G. S. Blimling and E. J. Whitt (eds.), *Good Practice in Student Affairs: Principles to Foster Student Learning.* San Francisco: Jossey-Bass, 1999.

Sadker, M., and Sadker, D. M. *Teachers, Schools, and Society.* New York: Random House, 1988.

Vaill, P. B. *Learning as a Way of Being: Strategies for Survival in a World of Permanent White Water.* San Francisco: Jossey-Bass, 1996.

Wingspread Group on Higher Education. *An American Imperative: Higher Expectations for Higher Education.* Racine, Wis.: Johnson Foundation, 1993.

Young, R. B. "Guiding Values and Philosophy." In S. R. Komives and D. B. Woodard, Jr. (eds.), *Student Services: A Handbook for the Profession.* (3rd ed.) San Francisco: Jossey-Bass, 1996.

**5**

*This chapter discusses ways in which student affairs'
operating practices, structures, and strategies could
change to address contemporary challenges.*

# Organizational Change

The changing climate of higher education means that colleges and universities need to rethink their organizational structure in order to address successfully the challenges described in Chapter One. It is clear, moreover, that there will be continued competition for public dollars to support higher education. As a result, institutions will have to generate new sources of revenue to fund restructuring efforts and renewed efforts to address what Edgerton (1999) describes as the increasing public frustration with our institutions. Institutions are unresponsive, they are costly, and they exercise little accountability. The familiar ways of adapting to external demands and financial crises (for example, doing more with less, adding new programs to meet emerging needs, or trimming programs to generate funds to support new programs) only delay the inevitable. We still need to reorganize our institutions to increase productivity, to contain costs, to use human and financial resources effectively, and to demonstrate accountability through performance-based outcomes.

In 1994, the American Council on Education and the Kellogg Foundation began an initiative to understand institutional transformation and effectuate strategies for successful change. Just as no one organizational theory works for all institutions, no one paradigm guides us in undertaking transformational change. Several principles about transformational change emerged from this initiative, including the ideas that transformational change is deep, pervasive, intentional, and long-term; it is organic and requires holistic and integrated thinking; and it requires new approaches to student affairs, faculty development, pedagogy, assessment, and community involvement (American Council on Education, 1998). The key to real change is not incrementalism, as expressed by change efforts in bureaucratic organizations. Real change involves instead reexamining basic assumptions and either reaffirming or modifying them so that policies and practices can be brought into alignment with the core values and principles of the organization; this leads to employee behavioral change.

In this chapter, we address how student affairs' operating practices, structures, and strategies could change to address contemporary challenges while still preserving core principles and values within student affairs and within the institution. In the first part of the chapter, we review myths and heresies about organizations. Then we discuss organizational theories and strategies for transformational change. Finally, we give advice related to navigating and managing change to practitioners.

## Myths and Heresies

We believe that in thinking about restructuring a student affairs unit or division, it is important to think of the myths and heresies surrounding organizational change as a way of aligning functions and practices with core values and principles. A dominant *myth* is that *there is one correct organizational model for student affairs.* We believe there are some good organizational models and some not-so-good models. In fact, there is great disparity among organizational theorists about the best way to organize in order to accomplish organizational goals (March and Simon, 1993). To us, however, it is critical to understand the organizational principles derived from the good models and how and when to best implement them, given the culture, history, and climate of your institution.

Similarly, another *myth* is that *management techniques, such as Continuous Organizational Renewal (CORe) and Total Quality Management (TQM), are highly effective management tools.* Student affairs professionals frequently have turned to these management techniques to bring order and purpose to their work. It is assumed that because these management approaches have been successful in the corporate world, they will be successful in institutions of higher education. For at least two reasons, however, this is not always the case. The claims of the effectiveness and success of these techniques in corporate America are mostly without credible documentation. In fact, several audits of these practices (TQM and CORe) in major companies have produced mixed results regarding their usefulness (Birnbaum, 2000). In addition, because our purposes, cultures, and intended outcomes differ from those of the business world, these tools cannot always be applied to higher education without modification. Borrowing these techniques from the corporate world may be helpful, but we need to be realistic about how they can be applied to organizations of higher education and how they can work for us.

Related to these myths is the *heresy* that *student affairs practitioners believe that rethinking or restructuring an organization, division, or department is not productive and is a waste of time.* It often seems that a great deal of time and effort goes into these planning activities and little happens as a consequence. Much to our dismay, the prevailing belief is that professionals should be given the resources and then be left alone to accomplish the tasks assigned to them. When there is little follow-through, it is understandable that student affairs administrators see annual goal-setting retreats and strategic directions reports as time-consuming, empty gestures. However, this attitude frequently leads to resistance to change and to a reduction in the unit's capacity to anticipate and initiate change.

Another *myth* is that *managers need to be charismatic, visionary leaders.* Even though having visionary leadership may be important during different times in an organization's life cycle (Mintzberg, 1973), many successful managers are individuals who help build the scaffolding that will be used to achieve long-term goals, based on the core values and principles of the organization (Collins and Porras, 1997). Collins and Porras describe this concept as clock building because it is better, in the long run, to teach people how to build a clock than to tell them the time. Successful student affairs managers draw on the core values and principles described in Chapter Two to build a clock—to create new strategies and tactics to meet contemporary challenges. To effectively build scaffolding that will support student affairs long after their departure, leaders must be coalition builders who work collaboratively. "They [must] understand their environment, project the effect of their actions on the environment, and understand how outside forces constrain and influence an organization's activities" (Cohen and Eimicke, 1995, p. 129).

## Organizational Theory

It is critical for student affairs professionals to understand a variety of organizational theories and managerial approaches in order to determine for themselves what structures and approaches might be appropriate for their organizational unit and for their interaction with the larger university. Therefore we need to shift our focus from finding the best organizational model, management approach, or practice to considering, in depth, what structures, strategies, and practices will allow us to continue to lead from our core values and principles while at the same time adapting to a rapidly changing environment. In this section, we discuss some of the perspectives that emerge when we consider organizational theory and begin to address how these perspectives can be useful in managing change both in the institution and in a student affairs division.

Organizational theory describes the "delicate conversion of conflict into cooperation, the mobilization of resources, and the coordination of effort that facilitate the joint survival of an organization and its members" (March and Simon, 1993, p. 2). It is a way to understand "social systems of cooperation designed to enhance individual effort aimed at goal accomplishment and to explain how organizations form, function, and survive" (Hodge and Anthony, 1988, p. 17). Organizational theory also explains such processes as resource allocation, policymaking, personnel management, leadership, restructuring, and reengineering (Kuh, 1996). Yet each theory attempts to explain organizations in different ways. Contemporary organizational theorists Bergquist (1992), Bolman and Deal (1991), and Morgan (1997) use the concepts *cultures, lenses,* and *metaphors,* respectively, as ways of conceptualizing organizational theory and of providing practitioners with a useful framework for thinking about organizational structures and behaviors.

Morgan (1997) uses metaphors to help us look at organizations from a variety of perspectives in order to uncover a multitude of intersecting, overlapping, or parallel interpretations of reality. Bolman and Deal (1991) use frames and lenses to filter organizational behavior in order to see more clearly how organizations work. There are many benefits of using such perspectives when viewing organizations. For example, they direct attention to the symbolic significance of organizational life and show how organizations ultimately rest in shared meanings. In addition, they encourage us to recognize the relations between an organization and its environment as well as contribute to our understanding of organizational change (Morgan, 1997). However, it is important to understand that using any one particular metaphor or lens limits our understanding of organizations because we view them in a distinctive yet incomplete and to some extent distorted way. We gain more by applying multiple metaphors or lenses to one organization in that we can more clearly see the different levels, agendas, and rationales that are at play.

Bergquist (1992) uses the concept of cultures within the academy to see more deeply into the way an institution of higher education operates. He suggests "that culture provides meaning and context for a specific group of people. Culture holds people together and instills in them an individual and collective sense of purpose and continuity" (pp. 2–3). In essence, culture helps define the nature of reality for those people who belong to that culture. Culture helps us understand the behaviors, values, beliefs, and basic assumptions about people in each of these settings. It also helps us see how the history, values, and perspectives of each culture form the educational institution as a whole.

The concepts of metaphors, lenses, and cultures may shed light on the complexity of the institutions in which we work. They also may help us identify the differing values and perspectives held by different parts of the institution (for example, individuals, departments, divisions), the differing agendas of these parts, and the ways in which organizations can work to navigate complexity and to mitigate conflicts that arise when these differing parts interact. The usefulness of the principles and the advice for practitioners presented throughout the rest of this chapter are anchored in your understanding of the intricacies of how your institution functions. It is imperative that you use some framework to understand the behavior of your institution. We encourage you to further explore the different metaphors, lenses, and cultures developed by these authors and others before embarking on transformational change. In other words, you need to truly understand the inner workings of your organization for the application of these principles and advice to be successful.

## Strategies for Change

The following American Council on Education-Kellogg principles, adapted from *Redefining Success: Education for the Common Good* (Kellogg Forum on Higher Education, 2000), are areas for transformational change that may be used to start a discussion on how well your division embraces these concepts, to begin a formal assessment of your division, and to develop new approaches geared toward meeting the challenges and expectations of a continually changing environment. Regardless of the way they are used, it is imperative that the assessment of these issues and concepts is done honestly and with integrity in order to ensure a change process grounded in the reality of your institution, its people, and its culture.

**Be Reflective and Intentional About the Principles Espoused by the Division.** Divisional values must be understood clearly by all, and there must be a shared commitment to draw on them in all facets of work. The processes of setting priorities, making budget decisions, restructuring units, and designing new approaches must all be driven by the core values and principles that your particular division embraces. This may mean radically rethinking how your unit is structured, who does what, and what percentage of time is allotted to each person's responsibilities.

**Align Divisional Actions, Processes, and Operations with Professed Principles.** Student affairs professionals must check continually to make certain that their practices are aligned with espoused principles. This requires periodic program reviews by knowledgeable individuals both inside and outside the unit. For example, every three to five years, units could undergo an external review to determine if practices are aligned with institutional and divisional core principles. Reviewers could be drawn from faculty, students, and collegewide professional staff members. Ongoing internal monitoring could continue by asking a simple question before making decisions: In what ways does this decision support our espoused values and principles?

**Be Self-Reflective and Self-Critical.** A self-reflective and self-critical division of student affairs thinks about who (students and staff) is being served and who is being privileged. It thinks carefully about what programs are being offered and what decisions are being made. For example, if a student affairs division values affirmative action and multiculturalism, its hiring and budgeting decisions should support this value. If during budgetary cuts individuals who have been in the system the longest are protected while recent minority hires are released or not considered for promotion, then fiscal, hiring, and promotion policies are at odds with the core values. By being self-reflective and self-critical, divisions of student affairs can become conscious about whatever values and priorities they embrace and become intentional about promoting them.

**Acknowledge an Agenda for Social Improvement.** The successful student affairs division is clear about its role in designing activities for students that will deepen their understanding of civic engagement. Activities and programs are available to engage students in thinking and acting on the issues challenging today's society. This may include collaborations with the community, such as building houses for Habitat for Humanity or donating the belongings that residential students leave behind to a women's shelter.

**Be Intentional About Outcomes.** Student affairs professionals need to be clear about the outcomes we expect from the "student experience." Although we state that we expect students to develop psychologically and socially, develop cognitively and morally, and gain responsibility for self and others, little effort is devoted to assessing these outcomes. Nor do we typically use what we know about what impedes development to help faculty understand how we can work collaboratively in designing what Chickering and Reisser refer to as "educationally powerful environments" (1993, p. 454).Taking steps toward these collaborations by interacting with the wider campus community to discuss these possibilities can help us move toward intentional outcomes. In addition, it is important to use these outcomes to help us shape and reshape our practice through being self-reflective and self-critical.

**Give Learning the Highest Priority.** Although student affairs practitioners espouse learning as the most important outcome of the undergraduate experience, many of our programs and activities define learning narrowly, in terms of leadership opportunities or developing basic competencies. In addition, these learning opportunities are targeted for traditional-age students. We must look to design and collaborate with learning programs that are academic in nature and include all students.

**Foster Inclusiveness and Civility.** Too often, student affairs administrators find themselves responding to student complaints and difficulties without leaving time to think about ways to include students in the life of the campus and without helping students understand their responsibility as community members. Learning to be respectful of differences and to conduct oneself civilly in the face of conflict is key to negotiating change and conflict.

**Take Responsibility for Decisions and Actions.** A division of student affairs that professes to prepare individuals to lead responsible and serving lives must also be prepared to take responsibility for its own actions. This means not only looking carefully at what we do and how we do it but also taking responsibility for the decisions we make (both good and bad). It also may mean discussing with others why we make the decisions we make, taking responsibility for poor decision making, and not passing the buck. Leaders need to acknowledge that all decisions will not benefit all students, and they should strive to balance the benefits of various decisions to all students over the course of time.

**Foster Information Sharing and Openness in Decision Making.** One of the most frequent complaints among managers is "nobody told me." Communication and openness are key ingredients of a successful student affairs division. Practitioners should review continually how people are informed about issues and decisions and whether or not individuals have had an opportunity to express their views before decisions are made. It is a good idea to institute ways of communicating with both staff and students that is quick, clear, and efficient as well as to develop ways for people to follow up on the concise communications with longer conversations. E-mail may work well for the first, open appointments; discussion times, set aside during staff meetings, often work well for the latter.

## Advice for Practitioners

Perhaps one of the most valuable lessons that can be learned about organizational change is that by focusing on new strategies and practices, new organizational structures, processes, and roles will evolve to support and sustain organizational priorities based on the core values and principles of the organization. Student affairs managers need to think creatively about how to restructure a division, or a unit within a division, to effectively meet the challenges posed by the issues we have discussed throughout this volume. Transformational change requires discovering the best way to organize human, fiscal, and physical resources to serve our students while remaining true to our core values. To facilitate your using the previously discussed principles to initiate the change process, the following tips are offered to help you think through designing change within your institution. Clearly, some of these tips may appear to be designed to assist practitioners in negotiating hierarchical, bureaucratic environments, which may seem contrary to the purpose of this volume, which is advocating more collaborative, team-oriented environments. However, in most cases, divisions of student affairs that are moving toward these collaborative work environments exist within institutions that still cling to bureaucratic principles and must therefore effectively negotiate this culture as well as the emerging, collaborative culture.

**Assess the Environment.** Develop an understanding of the forces within the institution and external to the institution that may support or resist change. By having a thorough understanding of the environment before beginning a transformational change process, you will find it easier to identify when changes likely will gain the most support and when changes may face the most resistance.

**Seek Advice and Alliances.** Discuss proposals with trusted allies who hold different perspectives on the organization. This can help you fine-tune proposals and plans by incorporating perspectives that otherwise may have been overlooked. In addition, identify individuals and departments that support the proposal, and work with them to develop alliances in other areas. When you have the input and support of others before "going public," your concepts, plans, and proposals can develop in safe space. And remember, alliances run in both directions; be willing to support and ally with others in their work.

**Encourage Civil Disagreement.** Use allies and other supportive people to develop plans that make agreement easy and disagreement difficult without compromising core values and principles. In other words, use language that is inclusive and civil rather than exclusive and antagonistic. Immediately address concerns that are expected to arise, and be willing to compromise and make changes if they will not radically alter your objective (Tropman, 1998). This often can help in securing support from those people and departments that hold differing opinions.

**Link Ideas to Values.** All plans have values embedded in their design. Make these values clear to others, and be willing to discuss them with people who hold opposing values. Discuss how differing values may not be in conflict with your plan and may coexist (Tropman, 1998). In addition, when constructing plans, link ideas to the core principles and values of student affairs as well as to those held by your institution.

**Listen.** Create an environment where people are comfortable to speak freely; however, pay attention to discord when it arises, especially in informal gatherings. People are naturally resistant to change, so throughout the process, you may hear concerns from people who are questioning or who are not supportive of change. Be prepared to address these concerns, either publicly or privately, whichever is most appropriate.

**Diagnose Failure.** This strategy goes hand in hand with taking responsibility for the decisions and actions taken by the division or department. Risk taking is expected when initiating change, and risks sometimes fail. Be willing to take a hard look at why something did not work. Diagnose the problems and environment that may have caused the failure, and then determine whether or not to try again or to approach the changes in a way that may be more successful. Take responsibility for mistakes, and stay away from blaming failures on other individuals, departments, or divisions. Conversely, diagnose success also. Too often, we are relieved when all goes well and we have a success, but we spend little time studying that success to determine what really worked well.

**Understand Organizational Politics.** Contrary to popular belief, politics is not all bad. Some may even argue that all interactions among people are inherently political. Regardless of your views, understanding who holds the power in an organization and who can help you achieve success is critical for a manager. In other words, understanding the political systems at work in your organization and becoming a part of this system are as critical as having a good plan. Learn how to become a good politician and how to navigate the system by learning who holds positional power and who holds personal power; then do not hesitate to use this knowledge to attain your department's goals and to share them with others.

**Watch Out for Danger Signs.**  Pay attention to covert and overt warning signals from others. For example, if hostile questions are raised about why the division is moving in a certain direction, this may be a signal that others do not value this perspective. Allies as well as opponents may try to warn of the problems or issues that may be raised by these suggestions. Do not consider those who voice these cautions to be disaffected or uninformed individuals. In addition, pay attention to external or internal environmental shifts, such as changes in students' interests and revenue streams (Farson, 1996). They could be warnings of changes to come.

**Pay Attention to the Analysis.**  Good data are important, but well-interpreted data are better. Because data can be interpreted in a variety of ways, understanding how to make meaning of data is an important skill to master. Using data to support new directions or transformational change could substantiate these decisions for others.

**Watch Out for a Not-in-My-Backyard Attitude.**  One of the greatest myths of working in organizations is the belief that *if it's not in my area, it's not my problem.* In fact, everything that happens in an educational institution affects student affairs in some way. Keep informed on what happens in other people's backyards and assist where you can.

**Take Care of Business.**  While attempting to bring about real change, it is important to continue to provide quality service in the basic areas (Farson, 1996). This will help keep you well respected within the organization for taking care of business while simultaneously trying to improve services.

## Conclusion

The management of student affairs departments and divisions often is a complex and unpredictable task that requires thoughtful planning and sensitivity to others. At times, it can be quite chaotic and demanding in terms of time and stress because of the highly volatile nature of student problems and campus issues (Sandeen, 1991). Managers, especially student affairs managers, can make things happen by pursuing priorities in a planned way, thinking and acting strategically to implement plans, and making adjustments based on changing conditions (Cohen and Eimicke, 1995).

The student affairs manager of the twenty-first century must work collaboratively with others to achieve mutual purposes by understanding organizational principles, financial planning, sound business practices, and human resource principles. Understanding that there is no one right organizational model and embracing several models can help us think about complex issues and problems from a variety of perspectives. Accept that there is no one perfect management style but rather a multitude of styles from which we can draw in order to develop cooperative relationships for mutual purposes. Although these concepts may not be heretical, they may require student affairs professionals to shift how they think and to change how they manage.

The change process, especially transformational change, is a difficult one. Managers and staff members must have not only vision and creativity but also endurance, allies, clear goals, and a well-laid plan. Yet nothing is as rewarding as successfully building scaffolding and helping people use it to reach their goals. This process is full of risk taking, but it can be loads of fun. Taking time throughout the process to take stock of where you have been and how far you have come is motivating for everyone. In short, transformational change takes integrity—carefully balancing being true to yourself, the profession, the institution, the student, and the core values that embody the combination.

## References

American Council on Education. *On Change: En Route to Transformation.* American Council on Education Occasional Paper Series. Washington, D.C.: American Council on Education, 1998.

Bergquist, W. H. *The Four Cultures of the Academy: Insights and Strategies for Improving Leadership in Collegiate Organizations.* San Francisco: Jossey-Bass, 1992.

Birnbaum, R. "The Life Cycle of Academic Management Fads." *Journal of Higher Education,* Jan.–Feb. 2000, 71(1), 1–16.

Bolman, L. G., and Deal, T. E. *Reframing Organizations: Artistry, Choice, and Leadership.* San Francisco: Jossey-Bass, 1991.

Chickering, A. W., and Reisser, L. *Education and Identity.* San Francisco: Jossey-Bass, 1993.

Cohen, S., and Eimicke, W. *The New Effective Public Manager: Achieving Success in a Changing Government.* (2nd ed.) San Francisco: Jossey-Bass, 1995.

Collins, J. C., and Porras, J. I. *Built to Last: Successful Habits of Visionary Companies.* New York: HarperBusiness, 1997.

Edgerton, R. "Education White Paper." Available on the Pew Charitable Trust Web site [http://www.pewtrusts.com]. Retrieved Sept. 2, 1999.

Farson, R. *Management of the Absurd: Paradoxes in Leadership.* New York: Simon & Schuster, 1996.

Hodge, B. J., and Anthony, W. P. *Organization Theory.* (3rd ed.) Needham Heights, Mass.: Allyn & Bacon, 1988.

Kellogg Forum on Higher Education. *Redefining Success: Education for the Common Good.* Unpublished working draft, 2000.

Kuh, G. D. "Organizational Theory." In S. R. Komives and D. B. Woodard, Jr. (eds.), *Student Services: A Handbook for the Profession.* (3rd ed.) San Francisco: Jossey-Bass, 1996.

March, J. G., and Simon, H. A. *Organizations.* (2nd ed.) Cambridge, Mass.: Blackwell, 1993.

Mintzberg, H. *The Nature of Managerial Work.* New York: HarperCollins, 1973.

Morgan, G. *Images of Organization.* (2nd ed.) Thousand Oaks, Calif.: Sage, 1997.

Sandeen, A. *The Chief Student Affairs Officer: Leader, Manager, Mediator, Educator.* San Francisco: Jossey-Bass, 1991.

Tropman, J. E. *The Management of Ideas in the Creating Organization.* Westport, Conn.: Greenwood Press, 1998.

# 6

*Financial trends and implications for student affairs and the likely new sources of revenue to support student affairs initiatives and ongoing activities are discussed.*

# Resources: Money Matters

The higher education financial woes of the past thirty years have challenged every sector of higher education to rethink long-term sources of funding for campus programs and activities. We had hoped that the financial turbulence of the past two decades was not a precursor of future conditions but rather a temporary condition generated by state and federal fiscal problems. The brutal reality, however, is that institutions no longer can rely on increases in tuition and—for the public sector—increased support from state legislatures and the federal government. Tuition has increased more than the consumer price index each decade since the 1930s for both the public and private sectors. According to the U.S. Department of Education (1999), between 1988 and 1989 and between 1998 and 1999, prices for both two-year and four-year public colleges rose 22 percent, and prices at two-year and four-year private colleges increased by 28 percent, after adjustment for inflation. It has been estimated that between 1988 and 1997 annual costs at public four-year institutions increased by just over half and at private institutions by nearly a third (Blimling and Whitt, 1999). In addition, higher education's share of state budgets has decreased from 8 percent to 6 percent since the mid-1970s (Woodard and von Destinon, 2000). This chapter focuses on financial trends and implications for student affairs and the likely new sources of revenue to support student affairs initiatives and ongoing programs and activities.

## Myths and Heresies

We believe that there are two heresies that affect our thinking about resources and several myths that influence our behavior and subsequently our decision making. The first *heresy* is that *student affairs professionals do not place a premium on understanding the financial and budgeting structure and processes of their institutions.* This heresy is based in part on the disempowering belief that student affairs professionals have been marginalized and have no voice in the securing and allocation of financial resources. The chief financial and academic officers are the "trolls under the bridge, and we have to accept their financial tyranny." This acceptance of a subordinate role in financial matters only reinforces the view held by finance personnel and academic deans that student affairs professionals have little appreciation for the complexity of lobbying for resources to support the institution's mission. Student affairs professionals need to develop an understanding of the state and federal budgeting processes, likely changes in financial resources, and the institutional budgeting process in order to become effective finance partners.

A second *heresy* is that *privatization and commercialization may be good.* Many of our colleagues view the marketization of higher education as "selling our soul to the devil," thus undermining our core values and turning student affairs into a McDivision of Student Affairs. For example, the privatization of a bookstore may be viewed as eliminating the value-added philosophy of the bookstore (that is, excess revenues used for the funding of campus activities instead of money going into shareholders' pockets). The reality is that the privatization of some bookstores has led to better service for students and to discounted textbooks and computers while still returning a percentage of the profits to the campus for funding student activities. Conversely, there are ethical issues that emerge that should not be overlooked or ignored because of the perceived financial return of these market arrangements. The underwriting of a campus recreation program by a local alcoholic beverage distributor may generate the funds necessary to continue this valued program, but it sends a contradictory and confusing message to students about leading a healthy lifestyle. The issue, however, is not so much privatization and commercialization as much as how we, as professionals, act ethically and protect our core values in the process of developing and managing these market arrangements that generate funds to support our work.

There are three prevailing myths about student affairs funding that are not supported by the data. The first *myth* is that *student affairs has been and will continue to be the loser in the allocation of financial resources.* In fact, the student affairs budget as a percent of the institutional budget has remained fairly stable during the past two decades—between 4.5 and 5 percent. What actually changed is the source and expenditures of funds. For example, under the Americans with Disabilities Act, institutions are required to provide basic services for students. As service practitioners, we have argued that this is important and necessary and is reflective of a core belief regarding the potential and worth of each individual. However, on some campuses, supporting mandated services has required shifting revenues from an existing program.

A second *myth* is that *all the money goes to academic affairs.* Again, in fact, what seems to have happened during the past two decades is that an increasing percentage of available funds has migrated to support institution-wide administrative functions and has gone less to instruction. Higher education instructional expenditures decreased from 32 percent in 1980–81 to 30 percent in 1995–96, while student services expenditures remained relatively stable during that time span (U.S. Department of Education, 1999). Leslie and Rhoades (1995) report that in private colleges the median rate of increase for administrative and support expenditures was 4 percent per year in real terms, versus less than 3 percent per year for academic expenditures. Moreover between 1973 and 1975 as well as between 1985 and 1986, the share of education expenditures spent for administration increased 2.7 percentage points for all public universities, while the instruction share decreased 2 percentage points. This reflects changes that measure in the billions of dollars nationally (Halstead, 1991).

The third *myth* is that *money drives quality.* How many times have you heard, "If I only had more money, we could have a top-rated program (or division)"? Money does matter but only up to a certain point (Bowen, 1980). In other words, there is a basic level of funding that is necessary for quality, but then other factors come into play that make a difference in whether a quality program is developed or remains mediocre. For example, in developing a true learning organization, as discussed in Chapters Four and Seven, the learning principles described (such as "learning is strongly affected by the educational climate") require a shared belief in the principle and—even more important—in the consistency of the principle with the core values of the institution. Divisional actions, processes, and operations must be aligned with professed values and principles. Additional resources will not make a difference in desired outcomes unless individuals believe in and are committed to the program objectives and work collaboratively with units outside student affairs to form these powerful learning environments.

## Funding Trends in Student Affairs

Little useful long-term data exist on student affairs funding in terms of sources of funding, changes in these sources, and expenditure patterns. The integrated Postsecondary Education Data Systems (IPEDS) is probably one of the best sources for this type of data, but it is difficult to disaggregate the data to examine trends and patterns. Nonetheless there are a few trends that are useful to consider in thinking about the future funding of student affairs.

**Institutional Allocations.**  As we discussed previously, the relative amount of money allocated to student affairs (student services is the budget category) divisions has not changed much during the past forty years. In 1959–1960, student services received 4.2 percent of the institutional allocations at public four-year institutions and 4.4 percent at private four-year institutions (Robinson and McKee, 1965). Similarly, for both public and private universities in 1980–1981, 4.5 percent of institutional money went to student services (U.S. Department of Education, 1999). Moreover from 1980–1981 until 1995–1996, a time span of fifteen years, the amount of money allocated to student services increased by 1 percent for private institutions and by 0.3 percent for public institutions (U.S. Department of Education, 1999). Table 6.1 displays the percentage of total institutional allocations to student services from 1980 until 1996.

In 1996, student service units in public two-year colleges received 10.1 percent of institutional allocations compared with 3.7 percent for student service units in public four-year institutions. As expected, the private sector schools fared a little better. Student services in two-year colleges received 12.7 percent of the college's budget, and student affairs units in private four-year schools received 5 percent of the institution's budget. Across sectors then, two-year schools received 10.4 percent while four-year schools received 4.3 percent (U.S. Department of Education, 1999). Together these data demonstrate that there has been very little change in the relative amount of money allocated to student services by institutions across sectors during the past two decades. However, what has happened on some campuses is that student affairs, as a division, has had additional responsibilities assigned to it without accompanying resources or has experienced enrollment growth without receiving additional funding.

**Grants and Contracts.** In 1990–1991, grants and contracts from federal and state governments constituted 10.8 percent of the fund revenue for U.S. institutions, whereas those from private sources constituted 5.6 percent of the revenue (U.S. Department of Education, 1993). Between 1988 and 1991, the percentage of institutional grant proposals increased from 14 percent to 19 percent (Davis and Davis, 1993). Grants and contracts have helped replace lost revenue institution-wide, and there is a similar trend emerging for student affairs. There is little national data on the growth of grants and contracts for student affairs, but a review of the literature suggests significant grant and contract activity during the last two decades.

Student affairs grant proposals usually are directed toward particular initiatives, such as health promotions, summer bridge programs, and student exchange programs, and toward demonstration projects, such as best practices on recruiting and retaining underserved populations. For example, since 1967, federal grants have supported TRIO programs, which provide services to low-income students, particularly minority students (Terrell, Rudy, and Cheatham, 1993). Contracts such as licensure agreements with soft drink or clothing apparel companies are becoming increasingly popular and profitable (Levy, 1995). These two activities have accounted for a significant increase in revenues for student affairs and have helped offset some of the revenue loss from state funding or other sources during the past decade.

**Auxiliary Units.** Another increasing source of revenue for student affairs is auxiliaries. Auxiliary services accounted for 10 percent of the fund revenue to U.S. institutions in 1990–1991 (U.S. Department of Education, 1993). Auxiliary units are those that generate all or a large part of their own operating budgets from sales or services (Moxley and Duke, 1986). Together these auxiliaries (for example, bookstore, housing, campus health, recreation center, and student union) generally represent 80 percent or more of a

**Table 6.1. Student Services as a Percent
of Institutional Funds Expenditures**

|  | 1980–1981 | 1985–1986 | 1989–1990 | 1990–1991 | 1991–1992 | 1992–1993 | 1993–1994 | 1994–1995 | 1995–1996 |
|---|---|---|---|---|---|---|---|---|---|
| Total | 4.5 | 4.7 | 4.7 | 4.8 | 4.8 | 4.9 | 4.9 | 5.0 | 5.1 |
| Public | 4.6 | 4.6 | 4.7 | 4.7 | 4.7 | 4.9 | 4.9 | 4.9 | 4.9 |
| Private | 4.4 | 4.8 | 4.8 | 4.9 | 4.9 | 4.9 | 5.1 | 5.1 | 5.4 |

*Source:* Data from U.S. Department of Education, 1999, Tables 345–347.

student affairs division's budget. Although this has not been the case for two-year institutions, auxiliaries are becoming an increasingly important source of revenue for community college student affairs units. Auxiliaries frequently are charged a surcharge or administrative charge for campus services; the money from these charges is used to offset other institutional expenses, including program costs in student affairs. It is also typical to charge nonauxiliary personnel costs against auxiliaries as a way of helping fund needed programs in student affairs.

**Outsourcing and Privatization.** Another trend that is emerging is that of outsourcing or privatizing functions in student affairs. Student unions outsource janitorial services and contract with vendors for food services. Some colleges have privatized their residence halls, bookstores, or health centers. Private companies managing these functions can achieve economies of scale not possible for colleges and universities while sharing profits with a college or university. The proceeds from the profits are used to fund existing or new programs in student affairs.

**Fundraising.** Fundraising is on the rise and is gaining importance in higher education in general and in student services in particular (Gordon, Strode, and Brady, 1993). According to the Council for Aid to Education (1996), from 1966 to 1996, there was almost a tenfold increase in current dollar support to higher education through fundraising efforts. The total contributions to higher education from all sources reached an estimated $14.25 billion in the 1995–1996 academic year. Included in this amount are funds from alumni, parents, other individuals, corporations, foundations, religious organizations, fundraising consortia, and other organizations. The funds that are acquired through fundraising are distributed in various ways. In 1995–96, the largest proportion of money gained through fundraising (55 percent) went to current operations, such as faculty and staff compensation, operation and maintenance of physical plants, public service and extensions, and libraries. About 45 percent of this money was directed toward capital purposes, whereas only 8.1 percent was given to academic divisions.

Student affairs is a newcomer to fundraising, and several student affairs divisions have either created a new position for fundraising or have shared a position with the institution's fundraising unit. Money is being sought to endow programs, to support operations, or to assist with building projects.

Donors are more likely to donate money if the goals of the student services unit are related to the donors' reasons for giving (Read, 1986), and students are often targeted as key players in fundraising pursuits (such as calling alumni to request donations). Fundraising will become an increasingly important part of financing such student affairs programs as leadership, service centers, scholarships, buildings, and housing.

**Partnerships.** Another trend is the active seeking of partners to help share expenses and to reduce costs. On campus, this happens, for example, when career services works closely with academic units to configure the best way to meet the career needs of students. Off-campus partnerships, such as high school outreach and mentoring programs or service learning opportunities with local service agencies, have increased dramatically during the past decade.

Pembroke (1985) and Garland and Grace (1993) encourage student services units to support initiatives that link private sector corporate America with higher education. This could then result in the creation of new opportunities or new programs that could bridge the worlds of academe and business. Examples of this include community service, mentoring, internships, and career placement programming.

## Future Sources of Funding

The traditional sources of funding for student affairs have included tuition and student fees, governmental appropriations and entitlements, auxiliary income, institutional endowment earnings, and gifts. These sources will continue to represent the majority of funding for student affairs divisions, but other revenue will have to be identified and generated to offset reductions in these sources, shifting institutional priorities, and emerging program needs.

The less traditional venues of acquiring revenue mentioned in this chapter, such as grants, contracts, outsourcing, privatization, fundraising, and partnerships, will most likely become more prevalent in the future as student services seeks to gain the resources necessary to deliver quality services and programs for students. Pembroke (1985) suggests that student services units should focus on acquiring mixed-fund sources of support. By relying on funds from multiple sources, units are protected from sudden disruptions if one source fails to provide funding.

## Implications for Student Affairs

The following implications are based on the underlying assumption that there is a great deal of effort necessary for student affairs to continue acquiring support from traditional areas as well as from new sources. In the midst of this effort, we must not lose sight of our core values; our actions in acquiring resources must be aligned with our values of fairness, equity, and holistic development.

**Centrality of Our Work.** Student service units need to develop strategies for demonstrating the centrality of our work to the institution (Pembroke, 1985). Our budgets need to clearly articulate the educational purposes of our programs. In addition, assessment and evaluation processes should be in place such that we are able to demonstrate, with empirical evidence, the importance of our work and the student outcomes that result from our programs and services. The link between allocated resources, quality of student life, and attainment of institutional goals must be demonstrated in order to relay the importance of continuing to receive funding for our units (Kuh and Nuss, 1990).

**Changing Our Role.** By becoming involved in acquiring funds from new sources, such as collaborative partnerships inside and outside the institution, student affairs practitioners will need to change their role to some degree. Our role increasingly will become central to and integrated with institutional roles and priorities. "We will move beyond the often isolated management of student life to a partnership with faculty and administrators concerned with the entire institution and its responses to changing conditions" (Garland and Grace, 1993, p. 51).

**Strategic Planning.** In addition, student affairs should engage in long-range planning with an applied model of systems budgeting. If not, we face the possibility of program and staff reduction or possibly the absorption of student affairs into other components of the institution (Williamson and Mamarchev, 1990). Included in strategic planning are the examination of current fiscal procedures and policies and the assessment and evaluation of our services to assist in maximizing the use of our funds. In the midst of decreasing fiscal support for higher education, we must regularly examine how and why our resources are being used (Pembroke, 1985). This is particularly important because student affairs units are among the most financially vulnerable in that they are often viewed as nonessential to the primary educational aims of the institution (Williamson and Mamarchev, 1990).

## Advice for Revenue Enhancing

Student affairs professionals may be more inclined to and familiar with effective advocacy in campus issues than in campus finance. It is increasingly important, however, for student affairs professionals to develop skills in the financial realm and to become active in identifying and advocating for creative financial approaches to the dilemma of shrinking and shifting sources of revenue.

**Knowing Your Stuff.** There is no substitute for being well informed. Get on the Internet and search the national databases on financial trends in higher education; the IPEDS databases are particularly useful in this regard. Learn about what your financial personnel are reading, and read their material. Keep yourself and other student affairs professionals informed about financial trends and issues. This will make you a well-informed participant in campus discussions, which will lead to richer discussions and more informed decisions.

**Collaborative Management.** Management is about working collaboratively with campus colleagues to achieve mutual purposes—working with other student affairs practitioners in developing an understanding of the financial and budgetary issues and constraints. Develop an open process for discussion about setting priorities as well as about resource allocation. Agree on principles for the allocation of funds, such as attaining consistency between the activity and the divisional mission and priorities.

**Options.** Seek alternate ways to fund and support existing or new programs. Ask whether or not there is another way to achieve the objective while controlling costs and successfully achieving the desired outcome. For example, community college transfer students have very different needs from traditional residential students. How can those needs best be understood and met without simply adding new resources? Some restructuring of existing programs and partnering with local community colleges may help achieve this objective.

**Who Benefits?** Always think about this. In the allocation of resources, are some students benefiting at the expense of others? Is the allocation of funds consistent with the principles of access, holistic development, and responsibility for self?

**Student as Learner, Not Customer.** Treating the student as customer leads to buying into the customer marketplace mentality. We forget to view students as learners and begin to think of them as customers, and our actions are designed to satisfy the customer needs of our students rather than the educational needs. Lead from our core values while trying to develop new funding and program strategies to meet emerging needs.

**Partnerships.** Developing partnerships is a powerful strategy for benefiting from multiple perspectives and for sharing costs. More important, partnerships provide avenues through which desired student outcomes may be achieved. For student affairs, partnerships with schools and businesses create opportunities for college readiness and transition programs, community service and student tutoring-mentoring programs, student internships, and career-related services. We need to develop and support partnerships in order to assist students in bridging the worlds of academe and business.

**Bottom Line.** Too often, we are willing to sacrifice quality and core values in order to meet budgetary requirements. Leslie and Fretwell (1995) state that "a major difference in value systems is driving a wedge between what colleges and universities do and what consumers and supporters want" (p. 7). In effect, student services units are experiencing a crisis of values, not just of resources. Higher education in general and student affairs in particular must not change traditional beliefs and values based on fiscal concerns but should become more conscious of these beliefs and values and of their impact on students.

## Conclusion

Fiscal concerns will continue to challenge institutions of higher education and will affect the financing of student services initiatives. Institutional allocations to student services most likely will remain stable, the acquisition of grants and contracts probably will increase, new partnerships will be formed, and auxiliary units will proliferate. In addition, outsourcing, privatization, and fundraising will become increasingly familiar terms in the field of student affairs.

By becoming aware of current fiscal trends, critiquing our thinking about financial matters, and attempting to find new sources of revenue for the future, we, as student affairs practitioners, will be better able to anticipate and proactively address resource-related concerns. We need to realize the impact of finances on the nature of the work that we do as well as on the nature of our role in the higher education community. We need to actively engage in the type of strategic planning that examines our current fiscal processes as well as the quality of our services. In attempting to survive the financial stress faced by the entire higher education community, we must not lose sight of our mission and values and must attempt to maintain a high level of quality in all that we offer to students.

## References

Blimling, G. S., and Whitt, E. J. (eds.). *Good Practice in Student Affairs: Principles to Foster Student Learning.* San Francisco: Jossey-Bass, 1999.

Bowen, H. R. *The Costs of Higher Education: How Much Do Colleges and Universities Spend per Student and How Much Should They Spend?* San Francisco: Jossey-Bass, 1980. (ED 207 368)

Council for Aid to Education. *Voluntary Support of Education 1996.* New York: Council for Aid to Education, 1996.

Davis, J. L., and Davis, S. K. "Involvement of Student Affairs Administrators in Grant-Writing Activities." In M. C. Terrell and J. A. Gold (eds.), *New Roles for Educational Fundraising and Institutional Advancement.* New Directions for Student Services, no. 63. San Francisco: Jossey-Bass, 1993.

Garland, P. H., and Grace, T. W. *New Perspectives for Student Affairs Professionals: Evolving Realities, Responsibilities, and Roles.* ASHE-ERIC Higher Education Report no. 7. Washington, D.C.: School of Education and Human Development, George Washington University, 1993.

Gordon, S. E., Strode, C. B., and Brady, R. M. "Student Affairs and Educational Fundraising: The First Critical Step." In M. C. Terrell and J. A. Gold (eds.), *New Roles for Educational Fundraising and Institutional Advancement.* New Directions for Student Services, no. 63. San Francisco: Jossey-Bass, 1993.

Halstead, K. *Higher Education Revenues and Expenditures.* Washington, D.C.: Research Associates of Washington, 1991.

Kuh, G. D., and Nuss, E. M. "Evaluating Financial Management in Student Affairs." In J. H. Schuh (ed.), *Financial Management for Student Affairs Administrators.* Alexandria, Va.: American College Personnel Association, 1990.

Leslie, D. W., and Fretwell, E. K., Jr. "The New 'New Depression': Enhancing Quality in a Time of Fiscal Stress." Paper presented at the annual forum of the Association for Institutional Research, Boston, May 1995.

Leslie, L. L., and Rhoades, G. "Rising Administrative Costs: Seeking Explanations." *Journal of Higher Education,* 1995, 66(2), 187–212.

Levy, S. R. "Sources of Current and Future Funding." In D. B. Woodard, Jr. (ed.), *Budgeting as a Tool for Policy in Student Affairs.* New Directions for Student Services, no. 70. San Francisco: Jossey-Bass, 1995.

Moxley, L. S., and Duke, B. W. "Setting Priorities for Student Affairs Programs for Budgetary Purposes: A Case Study." *National Association of Student Personnel Administrators Journal,* 1986, 23(4), 21–28.

Pembroke, W. J. "Fiscal Constraints on Program Development." In M. J. Barr and L. A. Keating (eds.), *Developing Effective Student Services Programs.* San Francisco: Jossey-Bass, 1985.

Read, P. E. *Foundation Fundamentals.* New York: Foundation Center, 1986.

Robinson, D. W., and McKee, R. C. "Expenditures for Student Services in Higher Education." *Journal of College Student Personnel,* 1965, 6(5) 259–262.

Terrell, M. C., Rudy, D. E., and Cheatham, H. E. "The Role of External Funding for Cultural Diversity Programming." In M. C. Terrell and J. A. Gold (eds.), *New Roles for Educational Fundraising and Institutional Advancement.* New Directions for Student Services, no. 63. San Francisco: Jossey-Bass, 1993.

U.S. Department of Education, National Center for Education Statistics, Office of Educational Research and Improvement. *Digest of Education Statistics.* Washington D.C.: U.S. Department of Education, 1993.

U.S. Department of Education, National Center for Education Statistics, Office of Educational Research and Improvement. *Digest of Education Statistics.* Washington D.C.: U.S. Department of Education, 1999.

Williamson, M. L., and Mamarchev, H. L. "A Systems Approach to Financial Management in Student Affairs." *National Association of Student Personnel Administrators Journal,* 1990, 27(3), 199–205.

Woodard, D. B., Jr., and von Destinon, M. "Budgeting and Fiscal Management." In M. J. Barr, M. K. Desler, and Associates (eds.), *The Handbook of Student Affairs Administration.* (2nd ed.) San Francisco: Jossey-Bass, 2000.

This chapter describes and encourages active, collaborative leadership from student affairs professionals to help reshape structures and processes in higher education so that they become more resilient and flexible in times of rapid change.

# Leadership

The rapid, complex changes evidenced in the trends identified in Chapter One have forced higher education to examine traditional practices that promote only slow, incremental change. Most higher education institutions have to deal with the paradox of being deep, enduring cultures while concurrently being contemporary, forward-thinking, organizations capable of leading in times of rapid change.

The pace of change and the complexity of today's trends pose adaptive challenges (Heifetz, 1994) to higher education organizations. These adaptive challenges require organizations and all organizational leaders to use new strategies and new ways of learning together to do this adaptive work. "Adaptive work is required when our deeply held beliefs are challenged, when the values that made us successful become less relevant, and when legitimate yet competing perspectives emerge" (Heifetz and Laurie, 1997, p. 124).

This chapter explores the shift from focusing on leaders to focusing on leadership. It addresses individual and organizational efficacy as well as the expanding capacity for leadership in organizations.

## Defining Leadership

Words like leaders and followers become burdensome and constraining in future organizations. No amount of "re-languaging" will free the word follower to be construed as anything but passive; likewise no amount of re-languaging can free the word leader to sound like something other than the positional authority. Hope may reside in the word leadership. Viewing leadership as a "relational process of people together attempting to accomplish change or make a difference to benefit the common good" (Komives, Lucas, and McMahon, 1998, p. 68) shifts the focus to people together (in all their various positions and roles). Leadership is the process of applying the collective efficacy of the people in the organization to the adaptive challenges faced by the organization. Leadership then seeks to use the "collective intelligence of the group" (Heifetz and Laurie, 1997, p. 132). The group must become a resilient learning community, open to what it needs to know, how it needs to be, and what it needs to do to address these shared challenges. The collective efficacy of the group is related to but is far more than the sum of the efficacy and capacity of individual group members.

## New Ways of Leading

New ways of leading (Allen and Cherrey, 2000) shift our thinking of leadership from being a "leader-centric" phenomenon to being "larger than the actions of a single person" (Drath, 1998, p. 404). The complexity of today's world calls for new models of leadership indeed. "Any model of leadership in which a person is understood to be the leader and others are understood as followers may not be adequate to the complex demands of such a world. What seems to be needed is a form of leadership that actually engages differences and sustains them in creative and useful ways rather than seeking their resolution through conflict, suppression, or compromise" (Drath, 1998, p. 410).

Most of higher education has been bound by long-term cultural practices and has been less flexible than necessary to do adaptive work. Recently, higher education has started to examine the downside of the rigid hierarchical structures and practices that have led to functional silos and impermeable boundaries, which have made organizations less flexible, less responsive, and less able to work collaboratively with both on-campus and off-campus shareholders. Determining how to lead, how to relate, how to influence change, and how to learn together are new organizational challenges (Allen and Cherrey, 2000).

As we discussed in Chapter Five, it is imperative that those in the organization know that the organization can change. "Viewing an organization as changeable increases one's perceived efficacy to manage it, whereas regarding it as relatively uninfluenceable undermines one's beliefs of managerial efficacy" (Bandura, 1996, pp. 497–498). This efficacy is linked to new views of organizations. In the 1990s, new views of how things really get done and should be done in organizations led to the introduction of Web metaphors appropriate for both the Internet and the structures created by spiders!—metaphors that describe complex relationships and links, nonlinear causality, and "blurred boundaries" in a dynamic milieu (Allen and Cherrey, 2000, p. 8). As noted in Chapter Five, if we view our organizations with new lenses, we quickly realize that we have to reconstruct leadership processes to address more complex challenges.

Instead we too often perpetuate a myth that hierarchies are a given in complex organizations and will always represent chain of command, authority, and stability. Clearly, ways of organizing that create work groups (for example, departments, offices) always will be needed and may have hierarchical dimensions, as noted in Chapter Five. However, these organizational structures may be flexible organizational spaces that are more fluid and permeable, promoting more cross-function or teamwork, with authority roles functioning as facilitators of reciprocal relationships.

We must challenge a related *myth* that *only positional leaders do leadership.* In this new paradigm, traditional organizational positional leaders become facilitators responsible for getting the right people together to address important problems. Leadership comes from all around, is a group process, and is woefully underdeveloped in organizations. Those who hold out hope for a strong new president to solve all the campus's problems are sorely disappointed. Indeed organizational members need to embrace the concept that "if it is to be, it is up to us."

Leadership is a social construction. Views of leadership have changed over time as society and relationships have changed. Early views of leadership included "great-men" theories or theories based on the perceived traits and characteristics of those individuals as leaders. Early on, those leadership traits were constructed to be classically masculine, leaving little room for leaders to have feminine traits or to use communal practices. Indeed feminine or cooperative behaviors were identified as not leaderly. In an organizational context, prevailing views led to studies of leader power and authority *over* their groups of followers. Those views assumed that only leaders did leadership and that others merely followed. Group process concepts of leadership elevated the role of followers to participants in the leadership process, encouraging leaders to become engaged *with* followers to accomplish group purposes. Elevating members, indeed transforming them (Burns, 1978), initiated our current discussions of inner values and the importance of common moral purposes by shifting the view of leadership. Burns describes leadership as a reciprocal process among people who are working together to accomplish something (usually a change process). Positional leaders have become so aware of this shift that they recognized that their credibility, authority, and influence actually come *from* their group.

In Table 7.1, Drath (1998) illustrates that contemporary views of leadership have moved toward creating common goals and focusing on leadership as creating commitments in members. This requires those who are doing leadership acts (that is, leaders) to be conscious of themselves (that is, their worldviews, their beliefs, their motives). Drath also proposes that the future of leadership lies in our realizing that leadership comes from all around, that leadership is a reciprocal relationship among group members who seek to make meaning together in their shared experience.

Although individuals can expand their capacity to come to the leadership relationship, the essential focus of our future efforts has to be on the

## Table 7.1. Evolving Models of Leadership

|  | Ancient | Traditional | Modern | Future |
|---|---|---|---|---|
| Idea of Leadership | Domination | Influence | Common goals | Reciprocal relations |
| Action of Leadership | Commanding followers | Motivating followers | Creating inner commitment | Mutual meaning making |
| Focus of Leadership Development | Power of the leader | Interpersonal skills of the leader | Self-knowledge of the leader | Interactions of the group |

*Source:* Drath, 1998. Approaching the future of leadership development. In C.D. McCauley, R.S. Mosley and E. Vab Velson (eds.), *Handbook of Leadership Development.* (p. 408). Reprinted with permission of Jossey-Bass.

interactions of the group. Recognizing that individuals may be very talented and their group may be dysfunctional (just think about many offices or departments you have known), our future effectiveness will depend on changing our leader-centric views to focus on *how an organization does leadership.* Understanding how the group (for example, work team, department, division) functions as a community of practice (Wenger, 1998), comes to learn together, and shares leadership in a true authentic way is essential. This mode of working must go beyond the annual staff retreat, the strategic-planning session, and the individual method of supervision. It is a way of being together in leadership all the time, which needs focused attention, reflection, and capacity building.

At a time when many viewed leaders as needing a set of skills or possessing a set of traits and viewed leadership as strategies and tools, Vaill (1989) wisely shifted thinking to the philosophies of leadership. Vaill used the term "permanent white water" (Vaill, 1989, p. xiv) to describe today's rapid change and challenged leaders to see that in times of rapid change, people cannot just work harder or longer, but people need to work smarter. Vaill challenged us to work collectively smarter, work reflectively smarter, and work spiritually smarter. These three simple elements embody the current trends toward new forms of leadership and will serve as a frame to present other concepts.

**Working Collectively Smarter.** Working collectively smarter requires a systems view of the organization (Allen and Cherrey, 2000; Wheatley, 1992). It means seeing the symbiotic relationships among offices and understanding that key processes such as orientation, academic advising, service learning, and strategic planning and issues such as attrition and developing key undergraduate outcomes cut across many units and need shared leadership among shareholders and stakeholders to address. Connecting these related people and offices brings more talent, more diverse ideas, and more resources to the goal of addressing the shared agenda. The best metaphor for working collectively smarter is to view our work environment as a community. In community, participants share responsibility for the greater good, and individuals feel some responsibility for the welfare of both other individuals and the community as a whole.

The wise scholar and founder of Common Cause and the Independent Sector, John Gardner, views communities as networks of responsibility. "All citizens should have the opportunity to be active, but all will not respond. Those who do respond carry the burden of our free society. I call them the Responsibles. They exist in every segment of the community—ethnic groups, labor unions, neighborhood associations, businesses, [academic departments, student organizations, administrative offices]—but they rarely form an effective network of responsibility because they don't know one another across segments. They must find each other, learn to communicate, and find common ground. Then they can function as the keepers of the long-term agenda" (Gardner, 1997, p. 5.)

Staff in higher educational institutions traditionally have functioned with low levels of interdependence. Too often, admissions marketing does not connect to student reality; physical plant work schedules have no regard for final exam schedules; student affairs retention interventions do not take academic advisers into account; faculty function as independent contractors who meet minimal organizational expectations (for example, turning in grades, meeting classes) and avoid citizenship obligations (for example, governance roles, honor board representatives, or group advising). Too little interdependence leaves the organization unsure if it has the capacity to pull together and promotes internal competition, not collaboration. Organizations that move toward higher interdependence will enhance their collective efficacy (Bandura, 1996). Collective efficacy is "a group's shared belief in its conjoint capabilities to organize and execute the courses of action required to produce given levels of attainments" (Bandura, 1996, p. 477).

Working collectively smarter means changing work expectations, reward systems, structures of task forces, and strategies for sharing information. It means developing staff to be boundary spanners and border crossers (Fried and Associates, 1995), able to relate to shareholders with different worldviews essential to shared, complex problem solving.

**Working Reflectively Smarter.** Reflection is the individual and group capacity to stand back and notice ourselves noticing. It is the process of seeking shared meaning from events, trends, and behaviors, which lets us gain perspective and be thoughtful about a leadership response. As professionally competent as student affairs professionals may be, it is *heresy* to assert that *many student affairs professionals prefer acting to reflecting and doing to thinking.* Student affairs staff often try to do too much in too little time and slip into crisis management modes. We are so consumed by metaphors like "putting out fires" that we do not step back to see the big picture. Making space in our individual and group lives for reflection is key. Every staff meeting should afford attendees time to reflect, to learn from recent experiences, to make meaning, to identify trends, and to forecast upcoming complexity. Standing back, viewing the bigger picture, and looking for emerging patterns in the ebb and flow of daily activities is what Heifetz (1994, p. 252) calls "getting on the balcony."

We challenge the *myth* that *extraverts—the Myers-Briggs Type Indicator (MBTI) E's—are the best fit with student affairs work.* Student affairs does attract a lot of outgoing, energetic, and socially oriented professionals who do fine work, yet the role of the MBTI *I's* (that is, the introverts) is essential. *I's* have been misunderstood to such a degree that an ACPA program some years ago on the MBTI passed out "*I*-ally" buttons to participants to show support for those with *I* preferences. Student affairs work needs wise professionals who are experienced with reflection; they may be the MBTI *I's*, who process and reflect continually as a way to regain personal energy and focus. Their personality preferences, which too often have been devalued in traditional organizational settings, are the very talent needed to help the group reflect, to bring meaning making to the forefront, and to value getting on the balcony.

Reflection expands our capacity for foresight. In *Servant Leadership,* Greenleaf (1977) projects that as time goes on, our failure to look into the future may be viewed as an *ethical* failure. Clearly, some of today's problems are the result of our failure to look to the future, to predict today's events, and to take wise actions when there was still time to act. If foresight is to be the *lead* in *leadership,* we must practice it together through reflection.

Reflection is essential to becoming a true learning organization. It is time we acknowledge the *heresy* that *higher educational institutions are not learning organizations.* Learning occurs in them, but the structures, policies, and staff practices do not promote collective efficacy for organizational learning. A learning organization is continually expanding its capacity to create its future (Senge, 1990b). The 1990s movement to examine how organizations can adapt to change and can increase organizational effectiveness led to an awareness of the need for organizations (that is, the people in them) to learn together. Traditional organizations that revered only top-down leadership and promoted control found those practices insufficient to respond to complex problems and address multiple perspectives. Senge captured this new approach to organizational learning as "the leader's new work" (1990a, p. 8) and epitomized this energy in *The Fifth Discipline* (1990b). Indeed others have advanced the concepts of leadership as the practices of those who facilitate how an organization learns. Vaill (1996) calls this "leaderly learning" (p. 121), and others connect the concepts as "leadership as learning" (Heifetz and Laurie, 1997, p. 133).

**Working Spiritually Smarter.** Working spiritually smarter encourages individuals to reach more deeply into themselves for the values, social consciousness, authenticity, beliefs, and faith that become their rudders through white water. Vaill (1996) observes, "In most serious uses of the word spirit, we are reaching for a word that captures our intuitive feeling of something that pervades, energizes, weaves through, infuses, saturates some person or action or thing or concept in our experience" (p. 215). The remarkable spiritualizing movement at the end of the century is evident in everything from community service to the resurgence of emphasis on character in business and politics (Conger, 1995).

Complex, chaotic times with profound shared problems require individuals and their organizations to identify the beliefs and assumptions that will guide their actions. Being congruent with those beliefs provides the integrity to create meaningful, trustworthy relationships. Individuals may know their personal beliefs, but organizations rarely have examined their practices to see what beliefs really are being promoted. How can a university say it values undergraduate learning but have no faculty reward system in place that implements that belief?

Working spiritually smarter encourages individuals to explore their inner landscape. Individuals can then acknowledge the transcendent connection to others that truly makes a community meaningful. Viewing groups, work teams, office staffs, our division, or the whole system as a community enhances the sustainability of the system. "Communities speak to us in moral voices. They lay claims on their members. Indeed, they are the most important sustaining source of moral voices other than the inner self" (Etzioni, 1993, p. 31). This moral environment then becomes one in which values are taken seriously and in which rich meaning can be made, knowing that the community expects to explore beliefs and principles as part of the sustainable processes of the community.

The three simple concepts of working collectively, reflectively, and spiritually smarter provide a useful frame to guide people in higher education organizations who are engaging in leadership.

## Implications and Advice for Practice

Practice can be enhanced by focusing on both the capacity that the individual has to engage in this kind of leadership and the processes that the organization might practice to enhance organizational capacity for leadership.

**Individual Capacity for Leadership.** An individual's capacity for leadership must be developed. Whether functioning in organizational roles with authority or without authority, effective individuals are self-empowered to know they matter to the leadership within the organization (serving as positional leaders, participants, collaborators, or followers). Individuals who will be most effective in the many contexts of leadership continually should heed Allen and Cherrey's advice (2000) and practice new ways of relating, new ways of influencing change, new ways of learning, and new ways of leading.

*Be Professionals of Character.* Individuals should expand their capacities to be professionals of character. Individuals who sustain long-term effectiveness know they have to be people of character, who value integrity and who promote ethical practices. They are keepers of promises and tellers of truth. They value the relational process and intend to be worthy of trust. They help their organizations learn to acknowledge myths, to identify heresies, and to clarify assumptions.

*Learn to See Multiple Perspectives.* Develop the capacity to truly see the worldviews, assumptions, and perspectives of others. The openness to learn from multiple views truly will bring together the best thinking of diverse people and diverse perspectives to address complex challenges.

*Lead from Multiple Frames.* As we discussed in Chapter Five and enumerate further in Chapter Eight, Bolman and Deal (1997) expanded ways of viewing organizations with their four frames—structural, human resources, political, and symbolic. Most student affairs staff view organizations through a human resources frame (Kuh, 1996), yet those most effective in organizations have the capacity to understand and to use multiple frames (Bensimon, 1989). No one frame is sufficient to understand the complexities of organizations, and promoting practices from only one frame limits the ability to influence the broader organization.

*Practice Collaboration.* It is not a myth to assert that student affairs staff are relational and value promoting healthy organizational relationships. Most are far better at cooperation, however, than true collaboration. Cooperation involves two or more entities coming together to meet each of their separate goals, whereas collaboration means jointly addressing shared needs or problems and developing shared solutions. Shared campus problems, such as attrition, underprepared students, budget reductions, and outcomes assessments, need collaborative practices. The attitudes and skills needed to be collaborative include being able to understand other people's perspectives, not needing to win, shaping a shared vision, and being trustworthy and trustful.

*Value All Meaningful Contributions.* Develop talent in the organization, and reward and celebrate the diverse talents that the organization needs to meet the leadership challenge. The introvert who helps the organization reflect and make meaning is as essential as the extrovert who gives the opening speech with great enthusiasm.

**Organizational Capacity for Leadership.** The leadership capacity of the organization must be enriched. In the late twentieth century, leadership practices shifted from focusing on the actions of the people who engaged in those practices to focusing on the relationships among the people in the organizations. Leadership in the organization is far more than the collection of the leadership capacities of individuals; indeed individuals must learn how to work together in leadership.

*Become Learning Communities.* Organizations should become learning communities. Organizations seeking to do so need to learn from their experiences every day. They address new challenges by asking what they (as a group) need to learn or know to address this challenge. They create a "culture of inquiry and dialogue" and promote a "spirit of inquiry," knowing that spirit is the connection between individual and team learning (Watkins and Marsick, 1993, p. 8). They know that true dialogue skills must be learned and practiced, so members can free themselves from old assumptions and enter into learning and being together.

*Promote the Organization's Collective Efficacy.* Confront organizational practices that diminish the capacity of the organization to empower individuals to work together effectively in leadership. Remove structural barriers; examine and advance policies and practices that encourage, reward, and sustain interdepartmental collaboration; and promote organizational learning and address the learning needed to face adaptive challenges. Assume that nearly everything important needs to start with an identification of core beliefs, values, and assumptions that will guide eventual decision making; would benefit with a cross-functional team; could be opened up for the advice and counsel of shareholders and stakeholders (certainly including students and community members); and needs serious assessment and evaluation to feed the learning cycle.

*Challenge Complacency.* Being adaptive and resilient means encouraging dialogue (for example, debate, questions) that keeps the organization connected to its core values and prime assumptions. Newcomers, whether they are the newly hired, the well seasoned, the department chair, the newest residence life professional, or the transfer student, have a keen perspective on seeing the organization with fresh lenses. Instead of embracing the traditional practices of asking them to "get the lay of the land and figure us out before you make any waves," encourage newcomers to "confront us on anything that seems incongruent with our stated values and help us see where we have processes and systems that might be constraining us from doing our best work."

*Look Ahead.* Develop habits and practices that keep a toe in the future. Becoming an adaptive organization means reflecting on trends and themes as they evolve. Even if the meaning of those trends is not evident to individuals, the group needs to pose such as questions as, How will it matter to our work if this trend increases? or How do we get ahead of this trend and shape our response?

## Conclusion

A discussion of leadership often quickly shifts to a discussion of the leader or leaders. Clearly, the philosophies, practices, and attitudes of individuals who exhibit leadership are important to an organization; those people are often identified as the leaders. Leaderful organizations, however, have many people at all levels and in all roles who take the initiative to work with others to accomplish organizational goals. New ways of leading acknowledge that traditional views of leadership happen from the top down but do not describe how leadership happens at all levels. Even more important, they do not describe the organization's capacity to exercise leadership as an entity. A department of ten truly talented, effective, well-skilled professionals may not function effectively as a department and may even be avoidant, divisive, and dysfunctional.

As stated earlier in the chapter, leadership is the process of applying the collective efficacy of the people in the organization to the adaptive challenges faced by the organization. Leadership then seeks to use the "collective intelligence of the group" (Heifetz and Laurie, 1997, p. 132). The group becomes a learning community (Senge, 1990b, 1999), open to what it needs to know, how it needs to be, and what it needs to do to address these shared challenges.

Today's challenges and trends, as presented in Chapter One, all benefit from new ways of leading. Our students and our institutions will be stronger, more resilient, and more adaptable if we promote organizational leadership capacities that foster the collective capacity of the organization through new views on leadership.

## References

Allen, K. E., and Cherrey, C. *Systemic Leadership: Enriching the Meaning of Our Work.* Washington, D.C.: American College Personnel Association and National Association of Campus Activities, 2000.

Bandura, A. *Self-Efficacy: The Exercise of Control.* New York: Freeman, 1996.

Bensimon, E. M. "The Meaning of 'Good Presidential Leadership': A Frame Analysis." *Review of Higher Education,* 1989, *12,* 107–123.

Bolman, L. G., and Deal, T. E. *Reframing Organizations: Artistry, Choice, and Leadership.* (2nd ed.) San Francisco: Jossey-Bass, 1997.

Burns, J. M. *Leadership.* New York: HarperCollins, 1978.

Conger, J., and Associates. *Spirit at Work: Discovering the Spirituality in Leadership.* San Francisco: Jossey-Bass, 1995.

Drath, W. H. "Approaching the Future of Leadership Development." In C. D. McCauley, R. S. Mosley, and E. Van Velson (eds.), *The Center for Creative Leadership Handbook of Leadership Development.* San Francisco: Jossey-Bass, 1998.

Etzioni, A. *The Spirit of Community.* New York: Simon & Schuster, 1993.

Fried, J., and Associates. *Shifting Paradigms in Student Affairs: Culture, Context, Teaching, and Learning.* Washington, D.C.: American College Personnel Association, 1995.

Gardner, J. W. "You Are the Responsibles." *Civic Partners.* Charlottesville, Va.: Pew Partnership for Civic Change, 1997.

Greenleaf, R. *Servant Leadership: A Journey in the Nature of Legitimate Power and Greatness.* Mahwah, N.J.: Paulist Press, 1977.

Heifetz, R. A. *Leadership Without Easy Answers.* Cambridge, Mass.: Belknap Press, 1994.

Heifetz, R. A., and Laurie, D. L. "The Work of Leadership." *Harvard Business Review,* Jan.–Feb. 1997, 75(1), 124–134.

Komives, S. R., Lucas, N., and McMahon, T. R. *Exploring Leadership.* San Francisco: Jossey-Bass, 1998.

Kuh, G. D. "Organizational Theory." In S. R. Komives and D. B. Woodard, Jr. (eds.), *Student Services: A Handbook for the Profession.* (3rd ed.) San Francisco: Jossey-Bass, 1996.

Senge, P. M. "The Leader's New Work." *Sloan Management Review,* 1990a, 32(1), 7–23.

Senge, P. M. *The Fifth Discipline: The Art and Practice of the Learning Organization.* New York: Doubleday, 1990b.

Senge, P. M. *The Dance of Change: The Challenges of Sustaining Momentum in Learning Organizations.* New York: Currency/Doubleday, 1999.

Vaill, P. B. *Managing as a Performing Art: New Ideas for a World of Chaotic Change.* San Francisco: Jossey-Bass, 1989.

Vaill, P. B. *Learning as a Way of Being: Strategies for Survival in a World of Permanent White Water.* San Francisco: Jossey-Bass, 1996.

Watkins, K. E., and Marsick, V. J. *Sculpting the Learning Organization.* San Francisco: Jossey-Bass, 1993.

Wenger, E. *Communities of Practice: Learning, Meaning, and Identity.* Cambridge, England: Cambridge University Press, 1998.

Wheatley, M. J. *Leadership and the New Science: Learning About Organization from an Orderly Universe.* San Francisco: Berrett-Koehler, 1992.

**8**

*This volume concludes by acknowledging that all professionals will need heightened skills and competencies to lead in these changing times.*

# Competencies and Perspectives for the New Millennium

As we hope has been made clear in the previous chapters, student affairs professionals will be faced with new and significant challenges as we enter this new century. When considering organizational and administrative performance, most of the traditional competencies that have contributed to professional effectiveness in student affairs will continue to be important for success. These include basic skills, such as listening, oral and written communication, and multicultural competence, as well as specific administrative skills, such as supervision, evaluation, motivation, planning, implementation, staff selection and development, and conflict and crisis management. One traditional, though continually evolving, competency—leadership—is so important that we have addressed it separately in Chapter Seven. As higher education continues to transform itself, these traditional competencies will need to be viewed and practiced in different ways. However, our focus in this chapter is on particular competencies that will grow in importance and on additional skill sets that may be required.

## Myths and Heresies

In this section, we identify some myths and heresies related to administrative competencies and perspectives in student affairs. Again, we state them as unsubstantiated assertions to make a point and to challenge the reader. The first *heresy* is that *individual initiative is just as important as collaboration or partnerships,* and it runs counter to prevailing student affairs culture, which has a particular focus on collaboration, consensus, and teamwork. We address this particular heresy in the entrepreneurship section and argue that in many cases individual initiative must come before collaboration, because it is often individual initiative that creates collaborations and partnerships. Competence at working individually as well as in collaboration is essential.

Student affairs is not a business in the traditional sense of the word, yet our concern, captured in this second *heresy*, is that *student affairs organizations tend to be administratively weak*. Student affairs professionals and programs tend to exhibit care and concern in their work and have particular strengths in the areas of individual and group advising, program development, and training. These attributes will continue to be important to our work as we enter this new century. However, with the continuing constraint of resources and the increasing encroachment of the marketplace, student affairs professionals and programs must also consider themselves to be businesslike and act as such. This includes discovering our "bottom line" through the assessment of learning outcomes and acting with the urgency of a business in organizing around those outcomes. In other words, we must begin to shape our efforts and behaviors in response to what we learn through outcomes assessment.

Related to this is the *heresy* that *most graduate preparation programs fail to prepare administratively competent professionals*. Graduate preparation programs, although typically strong in the areas of developmental theory and basic skills (for example, counseling, listening, advising), often fall short in teaching the knowledge and experience bases related to administering and managing complex organizations. In fact, the Council for the Advancement of Standards in Higher Education (CAS) standards for professional preparation programs barely mention administrative skills such as budgeting and finance. We argue that the student affairs profession needs to reflect on how best to incorporate important organizational competencies into the curriculum and experiences of today's graduate preparation programs (Garland and Grace, 1993). These competencies include those that are the focus of this chapter. Perhaps the lack of focus on these competencies in professional preparation programs is due to belief in the *myth* that *organizational and administrative skills are best learned "on the job."* We recognize that all skills are enhanced through reflective practice. However, just as developmental theory is an important foundational knowledge base for student affairs professionals, so are the administrative-practice knowledge bases. Even counseling-based preparation programs should at least ensure that students reflectively learn administrative practice through supervised internships.

## Emerging Competencies and Perspectives

Most of what we term emerging competencies exist in today's literature, and several may already be addressed in some graduate preparation programs. We argue, however, that these competencies will grow in importance as we move into the future. We also assert that particular attitudes or mind-sets, what we call perspectives, will be required in order to manage our student affairs organizations more effectively in the new century and to meet students' learning and developmental needs more effectively. The competencies and perspectives described in the following discussion are entrepreneurship, resource attraction, organizing around the assessment of learning and developmental outcomes, employing multiple frames of reference, technology adaptation and application, and futures forecasting. Most of these competencies are interconnected and mutually reinforcing. For example, it often takes someone with an entrepreneurial mind-set to be aware of the multiple ways in which they can attract resources to fulfill their entrepreneurial vision.

**Entrepreneurship.** An entrepreneur is defined as someone "who organizes, operates, and assumes the risk for a business venture" (*American Heritage Talking Dictionary,* 1994). In the for-profit organizational world, entrepreneurs risk capital and other resources, either their own or someone else's (that is, venture capital), on an idea intended to bring a return on this investment. The entrepreneur often is viewed as someone working outside formal organizational contexts and as a "lone ranger," who is out to serve his or her own needs. However, an entrepreneur in the context of higher education, as we describe it here, is someone who takes the initiative to address a problem, issue, or opportunity in his or her department, program area, or the institution itself and ideally works within a collaborative community. Pinchot and Pinchot (1993) coined the term *intrapreneur* to describe someone acting as an entrepreneur within the context of a formal organization. This idea is similar to but goes beyond the notion of a change agent in that this individual takes risks to make new ideas happen within the organization. The risks involved in this circumstance include reputation, cultural censure, and in extreme cases the entrepreneur's very employment. The skills associated with acting entrepreneurially also include other emergent skills, such as resource attraction (typically internal resource attraction) and employing multiple frames of reference. The entrepreneur who works within the confines of a university must be both a "rugged individualist" and a team builder. It is this balance between individual action and vision and collaborative engagement that makes these individuals successful. Clark (2000) contends that one reason why this conception of entrepreneurship is not accepted easily is that most individuals think of entrepreneurship only in the context of the business world, where importance is placed on individual gains and progress.

*Taking Individual Initiative.* Student affairs is all about community, community development, learning communities, collaboration, cooperation, teamwork, team building, and partnerships. As we indicate in our section outlining heresies related to emerging competencies, a concern is that student affairs culture has developed such a focus on collaboration, consensus, and cooperation that the role of the individual is often diminished, denigrated, or overlooked. Although we recognize the importance of teams and shared vision, we argue that there must be a stronger focus on and recognition of the role of the individual. In fact, many collaborations and partnerships are the result of individual initiative to benefit the organization—that is, someone put her or his values and principles into practice as an individual. This includes the notion of someone championing an idea despite obstacles, despite the fact that it is not a current priority for the institution or department, and despite the fact that others do not currently buy in. As indicated in Chapter Seven, all members of the organization must assume the responsibility of leadership. So even within a group-oriented culture such as student affairs, individuals should be focused on the skills and attitudes related to entrepreneurship. There are always situations when an individual must counter the prevailing norm or direction or when an individual must take the lead on an action and not wait for a consensus before making a move. We argue that student affairs culture can celebrate both strong collaboration and individual action.

*Being Proactive.* Becoming entrepreneurial involves becoming proactive (Clark, 2000). Colleges and universities are facing increasing pressures from their environments, and as the world becomes increasingly complex and uncertain, the demands placed on colleges and universities proliferate. We therefore must possess attributes such as courage, risk taking, imagination, self-confidence, creativity, and the ability to see the bigger picture. We also need the ability to see connections between institutional issues and stakeholders (for example, students, faculty, trustees, community members) that often go unnoticed. This involves seeking interest groups to engage in the entrepreneurial process that may have valuable resources to help build the case for the proposal. This, indeed, is working collectively smarter. We also must be willing to continue to cultivate the idea despite the criticisms of others. It is important for us to realize that coalitions must be created that cross boundaries, in and beyond the institution. In addition, follow-through and persistence are vital because there are bound to be obstacles, challenges, naysayers, resisters, and counterproposals, -ideas, and -plans. New initiatives do not grow in a vacuum; they grow in a context in which other things already exist and from which attention, energy, resources, and effort must be taken.

*Influencing Change.* There is no one method or process of entrepreneurship. Kanter (1983) presents a simple sequence of problem definition (acquiring and applying information to shape a feasible, focused project), coalition building, and mobilization (investing the acquired resources, information, and support in the project itself, bringing the innovation from idea to reality). Clark (2000), though not providing a process, does present five actions that a department or institution can take to make its culture more entrepreneurial. The first is strengthening a broad leadership core's ability to "steer" itself—that is, encouraging multiple individuals and groups to be innovative and proactive. The second is encouraging interaction across multiple boundaries—at the periphery of the department or institution and beyond. The third is diversifying the funding base of the unit by developing dependable lines of income from other sources. The fourth is encouraging innovation and proaction in the units of the organization that are traditionally least likely to act as such. In student affairs, it may very well depend on the institution as to which departments tend to be "stuck in their ways." Finally, if the unit addresses the first four actions, the fifth action of embracing an entrepreneurial culture will have been largely accomplished. All of these actions acknowledge that we need new ways of influencing change in our networked environments. The initiative to influence change can come from anywhere in this networked environment and does not depend on old notions of hierarchical authority. "The organic change approach challenges us to evolve beyond surviving rapid change to learning how to trigger organic change within a networked environment" (Allen and Cherrey, 2000, p. 48). Entrepreneurial competence involves the expanded capacity to influence change individually as well as to create and nurture an entrepreneurial culture—open to change and willing to take risks to enhance the student experience.

**Resource Attraction.** Most universities are plagued with constrained resources (Clark, 2000). Student affairs divisions tend to reflect these constraints and on most campuses often represent an intensified set of constraints. An organization existing in an environment that is perpetually resource constrained experiences inevitable consequences for the members of that organization. Ideas, proposals, initiatives, changes, entrepreneurial activity, and transformational plans all require resources if they are to be acted on. These resources include time, energy, materials, money, people, and so forth. In an environment where individuals are repeatedly told, directly or indirectly, "We don't have the resources," ideas are squelched even before they are expressed. In fact, they are squelched by the individual even before they reach full consciousness. Individuals learn—and internalize that learning—not to waste their own individual resources (for example, time to think, consider, dream, or plan) on notions that are dead ends.

In this new millennium, we can see the changes wrought by the shifting external landscape. The difference between public and private higher education has narrowed, in that public education must raise more of its funds through tuition and other sources to counter the decline in state support. Private institutions long have relied on external fundraising. During the past several decades, virtually all public institutions have followed suit. Even community colleges have created development offices and have launched capital campaigns. The ability to attract resources has become a key skill for any higher education administrator, and especially for student affairs.

The forms of resource attraction discussed in this section include fundraising, grant writing, resource sharing, and business and industry partnerships. Most of these were reviewed in Chapter Six; however, the focus here is on the competencies involved in each of these types of resource attraction.

Although the discussion in this section focuses on the money-increasing types, it is important to realize that resource attraction involves much more than simply capital or monetary resources and also includes human resources (for example, advisory boards, volunteers, new work teams and groups across campus), training and development, facilities, technology, and research development.

  *Fundraising.* Fundraising refers to the solicitation of funds and gifts from graduates, internal and external constituents, community members, and foundations. The purpose of fundraising is to help institutions and their component parts meet their goals and enhance the capacity to serve the needs of constituents (Brambach and Bumphus, 1993). In fact, higher education is in an age of massive capital campaigns, when even four-year public and community colleges are creating fundraising programs and setting lofty goals (Brambach and Bumphus, 1993; Miser and Mathias, 1993). Yet despite the increase in fundraising efforts, the student affairs division is rarely regarded as a source of fundraising or a driver of the fundraising process (Shay, 1993). Student affairs professionals need to challenge this notion both for the good of their institution and the good of their division.

  Graduates tend to develop loyalty to an institution through specific people and experiences, both academic and nonacademic. The challenge for student affairs professionals is to discover who the graduates of the student affairs division are and to identify those individuals who might be interested and willing to contribute their alumni dollars to assist with the work of the division. Certainly, any student who was assisted by the student affairs division is a potential contributor, but there also exist those students more closely associated with the work of the division. These include resident assistants, orientation assistants, judicial board members, student government leaders, and student organization leaders. These are the graduates to target as contributors to the division's mission and work. For example, Clarkson University has a resident assistant–head resident reunion as part of the annual university reunion activities and a scholarship fund that is named after a longtime residence life employee who passed away suddenly. The current timing may be right for such a fundraising campaign for student affairs divisions because most student affairs divisions expanded, formalized, and professionalized during the late 1960s and 1970s. The students who were resident assistants and student leaders then are now in their fifties and are likely to be in a financial position to consider contributing to the work of the division.

  An important task for student affairs professionals is to begin to develop a sense of an alumni community, a community that is connected to and informed about the ongoing work of the division. This can be done through various forms of communication (for example, alumni newsletters, e-mail contacts, and Listservs). Of course, before funds can be solicited, one must first know who the alumni are and where they are, so building a student affairs alumni community begins with the arduous task of identifying the student leaders and employees from the past. Most student affairs divisions probably have not kept this information on file. Even the alumni office may not be able to help unless, in their contact with alumni, they solicited undergraduate experience data. Probably the best course of action is to solicit student affairs alumni through alumni publications and then use these contacts to identify other student affairs alumni.

*Grant Writing.* Grant writing is a particular type of fundraising but distinct enough to warrant its own focus. A grant is a gift of money or resources that often is funded by a foundation or governmental agency and typically for a specific purpose. Foundations are nonprofit organizations whose purpose is to distribute resources to individuals and groups according to their specific mission. There are several types of foundations. For example, independent foundations are funded through individual or family gifts, community foundations are established in order to benefit community projects and organizations, and corporate foundations are established by business organizations for the purpose of addressing community needs. Grants are also available through governmental funding agencies for specific types of projects or programs.

Grants can be obtained for a variety of purposes but typically are sought for research projects or program development or enhancement. The purpose of the research or program must be aligned with the goals and mission of the granting agency. It is important for student affairs professionals to realize that there is money available to fund innovative projects and programs. Currently, there are more than 50,000 private foundations in the United States (Foundation Center, n.d.). This compares with 22,000 private foundations in 1980. In fact, since 1997, 5,200 new grant makers came into being. In 1998, private foundations (that is, those excluding governmental agencies) distributed almost $23 billion in grants. Independent foundations increased their giving by 17.3 percent during 1998–1999. Corporate foundations increased their giving by 22.2 percent during the same time period and by 44.2 percent over a two-year period. Higher education continues to receive the largest share of that funding—24 percent of all grant dollars distributed. The phenomenal growth in the number of foundations and in the amount of money distributed is due in large measure to the continuing strong performance of the economy and the stock market. Under federal law, foundations must give away at least 5 percent of their assets in order to maintain their nonprofit status, so foundations whose endowments are expanding greatly must give away that much more money.

Virtually every university and most colleges have an office to assist individuals in identifying appropriate funding sources, crafting grant proposals, and administering funded grants. Even if an institution does not have such an office, assistance in obtaining grants is available from a host of publications about grant writing and through Web sites, such as foundationcenter.com. Writing skills are important in the grant-writing process but more important are the initiative to pursue a grant to support a project or program, the idea itself, and the knowledge of the grant-writing and funding process. Taking advantage of competitive awards means knowing how to prepare a grant proposal to meet the specifications of the chosen granting agency. One needs a sound and convincing argument as to why a particular idea meets the foundation's mission and should get funding. A grant should be written to articulate effectively what the idea is, how it is designed to assist the organization in meeting its goals and objectives, and how the idea also meets the foundation's mission.

*Business Partnerships.* Partnerships between businesses and student affairs divisions are a viable, necessary, and emerging form of resource attraction. Although it is a fairly standard practice in community colleges and a growing consideration among universities, it is an area where student affairs has lagged. A business partnership is a relationship between an institution or individual program and a business that is characterized by mutual cooperation and responsibility, typically for the achievement of a specific goal. A partnership is not merely soliciting local businesses for funds, nor is it simply outsourcing (for example, health services, police and security) or contracting for services (for example, cleaning). Instead it is working together to achieve a common end in the form of institutional engagement. For universities in general, the advantages of partnering with businesses include strengthening business's understanding of and commitment to the needs of higher education through enhanced communication between the two sectors (Higher Education Funding Council of England, 1998). However, the partnerships can also yield much needed resources in many forms for institutions, including innovative ideas, new technology, monetary returns, service in kind, advisory services, and student placements (Utah Partners in Education, n.d.). One of the largest advantages of a business-university partnership is the potential to integrate working and learning experiences for students through internships, co-ops, and job placement.

Beder (1984) identified key components to consider in developing resource-sharing partnerships. The first is the degree of reciprocity between the institution and its business partner—that is, the balance that exists between giving and receiving resources. Another component is system openness—that is, the degree to which the institution is open to relationships with external parties. A third component is trust and commitment—that is, the interdependence between the organizations as well as the commitment to the partnership process from all levels of the organization. Finally, fluid and flexible structures that allow for adaptability and receptivity are needed. Forming strong, viable business partnerships demonstrates that the student affairs profession recognizes the importance of and understands emerging forms of resource attraction. Collaborative partnerships allow student affairs professionals to develop entrepreneurial skills through working with external constituencies in order to gain resources to further support initiatives and to increase student learning and development. Examples of such partnerships include involving area businesses in the construction or redesigning of residence halls in order to accommodate business conferences during the summer months or designing computer laboratories that also can be used as classrooms by businesses looking to develop their workforce.

*University Partnerships.* University partnerships are similar to business partnerships but differ in that the external partners are other universities, departments, or programs in other universities. In an era of constrained resources, it makes sense for institutions to work together to reduce the competition that serves to drain both institutions. One example of a major university partnership is the Northeast Ohio University College of Medicine, which is the result of a partnership among Kent State University, the University of Akron, and Youngstown State University. Perhaps the most common form of university partnership is resource sharing, such as the library relationships that have developed among institutions. Other partnerships can include cooperative course offerings, student and faculty exchange programs, combined professional and faculty training and development, shared facilities, shared technological support, interinstitutional research and planning, and collaborative student recruitment and admissions. Other shared services could include counseling, health services, activities programming, career counseling, and academic advising. Shared management is another form of partnership that could involve functions such as physical plant maintenance, health services, transportation, and security. It appears that for colleges and universities located in an area that is geographically proximate to other institutions, shared services and shared management functions are straightforward forms of partnership. Of course, with the expansion of the Internet, proximity is less of an issue for some of these services and functions.

Obstacles and drawbacks of university partnerships include initial cost inefficiency, due to the time and resources required to create partnerships, and professional tensions that may arise due to variations in institutional missions, organizational cultures, or administrative procedures (Konkel and Patterson, 1981). However, for most student affairs divisions, the obstacles to partnering with other institutions exist predominantly within the individual professionals, and perhaps the greatest obstacle to university partnerships is the perception of the need for competition among institutions and the fear of losing one's institutional identity through collaboration.

**Organizing Around the Assessment of Student Learning and Developmental Outcomes.** Student affairs divisions not only must provide various opportunities, programs, services, and activities to an increasingly diverse student population but also must seek to understand how these components affect students. The importance of assessing these outcomes has been stressed to student affairs professionals for more than a decade (Upcraft and Schuh, 1996). According to Erwin (1996), "Whatever the source or reason, professionals need to document the educational effectiveness of the programs and services they provide and for which they are responsible" (p. 416). This is done through what Blimling and Whitt (1999) refer to as systematic inquiry, which is "an intentional, organized, and ongoing search for information, [which] . . . must be valid, reliable, and believable" (p. 92). Systematic inquiry encompasses research, assessment, and evaluation and can be conducted using both quantitative and qualitative research methods.

For those student affairs divisions and departments that are assessing student outcomes systematically, the results are used most often to communicate to internal and external constituencies the value of particular programs as related to the academic and developmental mission of the institution. However, the results of assessments also must be used for another, often overlooked, purpose—to provide feedback to the program or department on how to better shape and improve services to students. This is what we mean by *organizing around student learning outcomes.* This means that outcomes assessment goes beyond the collection and analysis of data in order to assess the effectiveness of program organization, practice, and focus, so that it may be used to change and shape organizational practice. The New England Association of Schools and Colleges, an accrediting agency that holds this issue as a priority, indicates that the characteristics of effective assessment methods are structured, systematic, and ongoing; are related to other institutional strategic long-range plans and to planning and budgeting processes; emerge from and are sustained by the commitment of all institutional members; and provide explicit and public statements about institutional expectations for student learning (New England Association of Schools and Colleges, 1992).

**Employing Multiple Frames of Reference.**    The word *paradigm,* along with its cousin *paradigm shift,* has been used so much in our society, and especially in academe, that it has lost the power of its definition. The more widely it has been used, the more vague and diffuse its definition has become. It has reached the point where paradigm is used to mean an opinion or a point of view. The term paradigm as used by Thomas Kuhn (1962) in his book *The Structure of Scientific Revolutions* was a much more powerful concept. To Kuhn, a paradigm was a pervasive, subconscious filter through which individuals accrued information about, made sense of, and acted in the world. Paradigms are themselves invisible influences and make data outside the paradigm invisible; they shape the reality experienced by members of a society and culture. Spurred by Kuhn's work and the work of cultural anthropologists and sociologists, social scientists intensified their exploration of the influence of paradigms on the structure of communities, organizations, and society in general.

Paradigms are deeply embedded systems of meaning making, and within paradigmatic worldviews there are other subconscious, but less deeply embedded, meaning-making frames of reference. In addition to frames of reference, they have also been labeled *frames* (Bolman and Deal, 1997), *interpretive frameworks* (Love, 1995), and *perspectives* (Manning, 1993). There may be many different frames of reference operating in any particular organization. Love identified two distinct sets of interpretive frameworks operating within a department of residence life—an administrative interpretive framework and a developmental framework. These frameworks influence the perceptions, actions, and experiences of the people who hold them. Bolman and Deal describe several frames through which organizations are experienced—structural, human resource, political, and symbolic.

What is important to realize about frames of reference is that like paradigms they are subconscious, but unlike paradigms they are brought to a conscious level much more easily. Another difference is that paradigms tend to be shared widely by cultures and societies, whereas there are multiple frames of reference usually operating in an organization or subculture. Because these frames of reference tend to be subconscious, many people in organizations do not recognize when different frames of reference are being employed. This can lead to miscommunication and misunderstandings among organizational members. Therefore one of the emerging competencies that we propose is the ability to recognize and employ multiple frames of reference. This requires that we try to identify our own perspectives, viewpoints, and assumptions and learn from experiences where our perspectives are shown to be faulty. It also means that we are open to alternative frames of reference, are not defensive to alternate views and critiques of our own, and are willing to discover and learn from our own and others' mistakes.

Although multiculturalism is listed as a traditional skill and priority in student affairs, it is important to highlight this issue in this section because it involves the ability to recognize, to respect, and to learn from the multiple and varying perspectives that have developed in our society and culture around such issues as gender, race, ethnicity, sexual orientation, and socioeconomic status. Employing multiple frames of reference in this instance requires recognizing that our gender, race, religion, sexual orientation, and so forth influence to some degree how we experience and perceive the world around us. We need to discover these influences while at the same time recognizing the existence of the same influences in others and being open to discovering those. Pedersen (1988) addresses these issues in his three-stage Multicultural Development Model. Stage one is awareness: one becomes aware of oneself and others as cultural beings. Stage two involves the ongoing acquisition of knowledge and information about one's own and others' cultures. Finally, stage three involves the development of skills related to translating awareness and knowledge into action.

**Technology Adaptation and Application.** The notion of technology adaptation and application is less a competency than it is a mind-set. The days when the "techies" deliver hardware and software to departments, programs, or divisions and tell us how to use them must be eliminated. The sophistication of technology has reached a point where it can be shaped to meet the needs and expectations of the end users. It is important that student affairs professionals involve themselves in the conversations on campus in which decisions about technology applications are made. The needs and desires of end users must be voiced in these campus discussions. Web sites need to be shaped by staff expectations in order to enhance student service. Administrative software must be designed or purchased with students and staff in mind. Most student affairs professionals do not have to know anything about how to create Web sites. However, they should understand how students use Web sites related to their office's services. One does not need to know how a car runs to know what one needs to use it for, whether it is for transporting groups of children, hauling materials, or performing well in bad weather. The same principle applies to the new technologies. The tendency is for student affairs professionals to leave technology decisions to the techies. This is inappropriate and ultimately damaging to an individual office's ability to serve its students. Technological competence then transcends knowing mechanics to developing a mindset and philosophy "to capture critical, enduring principles, assumptions, and strategies that practitioners can use to promote student involvement and learning in a dynamic, ever-changing information technology landscape" (Engstrom and Kruger, 1997, p. 3).

**Futures Forecasting.** The cycle of change is so fast that we have little time to respond if we wait for issues to be on our doorstep. Broadening our field of vision (that is, seeing the big picture) is essential if we are to anticipate, shape, and influence the impact of change. Futures forecasting involves the competencies needed to scan the environment and to identify those trends and events that will influence student affairs and campus practice (Case, 1984). Futures forecasting includes such strategies as analyzing trends, benchmarking (Alstete, 1995), studying developments of comparable peer or aspirational peer institutions, and identifying possible scenarios (for example, How do our programs and services need to change if our evening adult student enrollment increases?) (Morrison, 1994). Futurist Howard Case (1984) clarifies that "an issue is an unsettled matter which is ready for decision. Trends, on the other hand, are detectable changes which precede issues" (p. 38). Trend watching involves tracking topics of interest in the media. The way that television, the movies, newspapers, music, and magazines portray everything from youth culture to the social action agenda will somehow influence higher education (Merriam and Makower, 1988). In addition to monitoring our professional literature in student affairs, we must connect with institutional-type literature (for example, land grant colleges, community colleges, independent colleges) and track trends in those documents. It is hard to imagine a period of time that has not happened yet, but we can develop skills to understand the future (James, 1996). As we discussed in Chapter Seven, student affairs professionals need to develop the capacity of working reflectively smarter. Making time in staff meetings to reflect on and seek the meaning of the trends and issues we identify, as well as their impact on students and student affairs work, is essential in these times of rapid change.

## Conclusion

Based on his study of five European institutions of higher education in the midst of transforming themselves to meet the demands of the new century, Clark (2000, pp. 14–16) describes collegial entrepreneurialism as a culture of entrepreneurialism. The "pathways to transformation" that he discovered incorporate a number of the competencies and perspectives addressed in this chapter. For example, his "strengthened steering core" of collegial leaders took initiative to address funding constraints and tried new initiatives whose outcomes then shaped further efforts. Clark put forth the notion of an "enhanced developmental periphery," which he described as peripheral units (student affairs?) reaching "across old boundaries, and linking up with outside interests." Clark's notion of a "diversified funding base" describes institutions no longer waiting for funding sources "to come to their senses" but instead choosing "to become proactive financially, seeking to develop dependable lines of income from other sources," which is reminiscent of our focus on resource attraction. He also noted that institutions that embraced an entrepreneurial culture internalized new perspectives regarding expectations related to the role and function of all members of the institution. In essence, individual initiative and entrepreneurialism in a collegial and cooperative context were expected, hence the notion of collegial entrepreneurialism emerged.

As anyone associated with student affairs can clearly see, higher education in general is responding to changes in and forces from the external environment as well as to changes internal to the institution, such as distance learning and changing student bodies. It is therefore important that individual student affairs professionals also consider how they need to enhance and add to their skill sets in order to meet the challenges of this changing world. We argue that the particular skills that will be needed include entrepreneurship, resource attraction, organizing around the assessment of student learning and developmental outcomes, employing multiple frames of reference, technology adaptation and application, and futures forecasting. By adding these to traditional competencies, student affairs professionals can look forward to enhanced effectiveness.

## Epilogue

Our desire in this volume was to stimulate and to challenge the reader, perhaps even to provoke the reader. The purpose, ultimately, was to get the reader to think about and to reflect on the material presented and to consider how what we present compares with the reader's own beliefs and experiences. Student affairs is a wonderful profession with laudable goals. It comprises a vast number of capable and caring professionals intending to meet the learning and developmental needs of their students. However, as with any other collective entity, inertia sets in and needed changes and improvements become difficult to see. The dawning of a new century provides an opportunity for a period of reflection during which we can look to and plan for the future. By presenting myths and heresies about the field, we sought to challenge any sense of complacency that may exist within the field and to stimulate the thinking and reflection we desired. We hope that the readers will reflect collectively with their colleagues to identify campus-based myths and to suggest provocative heresies. By presenting themes and trends, we wanted professionals to consider the world in which we exist now, and by identifying core values and principles, we hoped to provide the elements of continuity from our past that can be brought to the challenges facing us today as we continue the process of constructing our future. Again, we hope that the readers will work together with colleagues to identify the trends on their own campus and in their own sector of the United States in order to develop appropriate responses to these ongoing changes. Finally, we hoped to provide information about important issues related to the topics of each chapter, such as students, organizations, and our own competencies, in order to assist with the process of meeting our present and future challenges.

### References

Allen, K. E., and Cherrey, C. *Systemic Leadership: Enriching the Meaning of Our Work.* Washington, D.C.: American College Personnel Association and National Association of Campus Activities, 2000.

Alstete, J. W. *Benchmarking in Higher Education: Adapting Best Practices to Improve Quality.* ASHE-ERIC Higher Education Report no. 5. Washington, D.C.: George Washington University Press, 1995.

*American Heritage Talking Dictionary.* Cambridge, Mass.: SoftKey International, 1994.

Beder, H. (ed.). "Interorganizational Cooperation: Why and How?" In H. Beder (ed.), *Realizing the Potential of Interorganizational Cooperation.* New Directions for Continuing Education, no. 23. San Francisco: Jossey-Bass, 1984.

Blimling, G. S., and Whitt, E. J. (eds.). *Good Practice in Student Affairs: Principles to Foster Student Learning.* San Francisco: Jossey-Bass, 1999.

Bolman, L. G., and Deal, T. E. *Reframing Organizations: Artistry, Choice, and Leadership.* (2nd ed.) San Francisco: Jossey-Bass, 1997.

Brambach, M. A., and Bumphus, W. G. "The Fundamentals of Community College Fundraising." *Community Colleges Journal,* 1993, *63,* 14–19.

Case, W. H. *Issue Management: Origins of the Future.* Stamford, Conn.: Issue Action, 1984.

Clark, B. R. "Collegial Entrepreneurship in Proactive Universities: Lessons from Europe." *Change,* 2000, *32*(1), 10–19.

Engstrom, C. M., and Kruger, K. W. *Using Technology to Promote Student Learning: Opportunities for Today and Tomorrow.* New Directions for Student Services, no. 78. San Francisco: Jossey-Bass, 1997.

Erwin, T. D. "Assessment, Evaluation, and Research." In S. R. Komives and D. B. Woodard, Jr. (eds.), *Student Services: A Handbook for the Profession.* (3rd ed.) San Francisco: Jossey-Bass, 1996.

Foundation Center. [http://www.fdncenter.org]. n.d.

Garland, P. H., and Grace, T. W. *New Perspectives for Student Affairs Professionals: Evolving Realities, Responsibilities, and Roles.* ASHE-ERIC Higher Education Report no. 7. Washington, D.C.: School of Education and Human Development, George Washington University, 1993.

Higher Education Funding Council of England. [http://www.niss.ac.uk/education/hefce/]. 1998.

James, J. *Thinking in the Future Tense: A Workout for the Mind.* New York: Touchstone, 1996.

Kanter, R. M. *The Change Masters: Innovation and Entrepreneurship in the American Corporation.* New York: Simon & Schuster, 1983.

Konkel, R. H., and Patterson, L. D. "Sharing Collegiate Resources: Guidelines to Facilitate Interinstitutional Resource Sharing." Paper presented at the National Invitational Conference for Interinstitutional Leadership, Wingspread, Wisconsin, March 1981.

Kuhn, T. *The Structure of Scientific Revolutions.* (2nd ed.) Chicago: University of Chicago Press, 1962.

Love, P. G. "Interpretive Frameworks: A Qualitative Analysis of Individual Sense-Making in a Department of Residence Life." *Journal of College Student Development,* 1995, *36*(3), 236–243.

Manning, K. "Properties of Institutional Culture." In G. D. Kuh (ed.), *Cultural Perspectives in Student Affairs Work.* Lanham, Md.: University Press of America, 1993.

Merriam, J. E., and Makower, J. *Trend Watching.* New York: AMACOM, 1988.

Miser, K. M., and Mathias, T. D. "Creating a Student Affairs Institution Advancement Program: Strategies for Success." In M. C. Terrell and J. A. Gold (eds.), *New Roles for Educational Fundraising and Institutional Advancement.* New Directions for Student Services, no. 63. San Francisco: Jossey-Bass, 1993.

Morrison, I. *Future Tense.* New York: Morrow, 1994.

New England Association of Schools and Colleges. "Policy on Institutional Effectiveness." [http://www.neasc.org/cihe/instuteffect.htm]. 1992.

Pedersen, P. *Handbook for Developing Multicultural Awareness.* Alexandria, Va.: American Association of Counseling and Development, 1988.

Pinchot, G., and Pinchot, E. *The End of Bureaucracy and the Rise of the Intelligent Organization.* San Francisco: Berrett-Koehler, 1993.

Shay, J. E. "The President's Perspective on Student Affairs and Educational Fundraising." In M. C. Terrell and J. A. Gold (eds.), *New Roles for Educational Fundraising and Institutional Advancement.* New Directions for Student Services, no. 63. San Francisco: Jossey-Bass, 1993.

Upcraft, M. L., and Schuh, J. H. *Assessment in Student Affairs: A Guide for Practitioners.* San Francisco: Jossey-Bass, 1996.

Utah Partners in Education. [http://www.utahpartnership.utah.org]. n.d.

# INDEX

# Back Issue/Subscription Order Form

Copy or detach and send to:
**Jossey-Bass Publishers, 350 Sansome Street, San Francisco CA 94104-1342**

Call or fax toll free!
**Phone 888-378-2537 6AM–5PM PST; Fax 800-605-2665**

Back issues: Please send me the following issues at $23 each
(Important: please include series initials and issue number, such as SS90)

1. SS _____

_____

_____

$ _____ Total for single issues

$ _____ Shipping charges (for single issues *only;* subscriptions are exempt
from shipping charges): Up to $30, add $5$^{50}$ • $30$^{01}$–$50, add $6$^{50}$
$50$^{01}$–$75, add $8 • $75$^{01}$–$100, add $10 • $100$^{01}$–$150, add $12
Over $150, call for shipping charge

Subscriptions Please ❑ start ❑ renew my subscription to *New Directions for
Student Services* for the year _____ at the following rate:

U.S. ❑ Individual $58 ❑ Institutional $104
Canada: ❑ Individual $83 ❑ Institutional $129
All Others: ❑ Individual $88 ❑ Institutional $134

**NOTE:** Subscriptions are quarterly, and are for the calendar year only.
Subscriptions begin with the Spring issue of the year indicated above.

$ _____ Total single issues and subscriptions (Add appropriate sales tax for
your state for single issue orders. No sales tax for U.S. subscriptions. NY
and Canadian residents, add GST for subscriptions and single issues.)

❑ Payment enclosed (U.S. check or money order only)
❑ VISA, MC, AmEx, Discover Card #_____ Exp. date_____

Signature _____ Day phone _____
❑ Bill me (U.S. institutional orders only. Purchase order required.)
Purchase order #_____
Federal Tax ID 135593032   GST 89102-8052

Name _____

Address _____

_____

Phone_____ E-mail _____

For more information about Jossey-Bass Publishers, visit our Web site at:
www.josseybass.com   **PRIORITY CODE = ND1**